THIS JOURNAL BELONGS TO

_____

_____

If found, I would appreciate its return!

PAM
LARICCHIA

The UNSCHOOLING JOURNEY

A FIELD GUIDE

Illustrated by Hema Bharadwaj

ISBN: 978-0-9940555-5-2

Published by Forever Curious Press

Illustrated by Hema Bharadwaj
Edited by Alexandra Peace
Cover and Interior Design by JD Smith

Joseph Campbell's Hero's Journey schema from *The Hero with a Thousand Faces*
(New World Library) copyright © 2008 by the Joseph Campbell Foundation (jcf.org),
used with permission.

forevercuriouspress.com

CONTENTS

For my children,
who continue to inspire me to keep an open mind.

HOW TO USE THIS BOOK

I am excited to invite you to document your own journey alongside mine! You will find both lined and blank sections throughout the book, space meant for you to write about your experiences, clarify your thoughts, and to doodle or sketch whatever comes to mind. You will also find colouring pages—beautiful illustrations by Hema, an unschooling parent herself—created specifically to visually reflect the inner journey we are taking as we embrace unschooling. You can check out more of her work at www.hemabharadwaj.com.

Please feel free to play in these pages and create a journal that is uniquely yours.

And if at times you are feeling flustered or lost, maybe look back over your notes to remind yourself how far you've come. You just might inspire yourself to keep moving forward!

INTRODUCTION

THE HERO'S JOURNEY.

I am thrilled you've chosen to join me in exploring the landmarks and features of the journey to unschooling. Our path may be fraught with perilous cliff-top trails and fast flowing waters, but we will also find safe harbours where we can rest and lush lowlands where we'll find nourishing foods to replenish our strength.

Yet for all its wildness and surprises, we are not the first to venture on this kind of epic journey into a new world. Human history is an intricate patchwork of heroic stories: European fairy tales of princesses and witches; ancient Greek myths featuring Zeus and Heracles; stories from religious traditions such as those of Mohammed, Jesus, and Guatama Buddha; the rituals and tales from Indigenous communities in the Americas, Australia, and Africa; and familiar, modern epics such as George Lucas' Star Wars and JK Rowling's Harry Potter.

These seemingly disparate stories have grown from the same roots: what it means to be a human being living fully in the world—growing older and wiser. Joseph Campbell (1904–1987), an avid mythologist, spent years collecting and analyzing countless stories from around the world. The result was his influential book, *The Hero with a Thousand Faces* (published in 1949). He discovered an underlying pattern at the heart of heroic stories from across all cultures and eras, and he called it the monomyth—the general sequence of events that outlines the hero's journey.

THE UNSCHOOLING PARENT AS HERO

How does this sequence of events relate to the journey to unschooling that we are about to undertake?

The monomyth of the hero describes an individual who somehow stumbles upon clues to a truth that lies outside of conventional belief, and begins a quest—physical, spiritual, or both—to understand and eventually embody that truth as their new way of life.

Sound familiar? Unschooling, which I broadly define as learning without a curriculum, lies unquestionably beyond today's conventional wisdom about learning, parenting, and childhood. And through our journey to understand unschooling, we will learn and grow and change as we come to embrace this new lifestyle. Ours will be an inner, or spiritual, journey, but it will no less powerful for it. By the end, we will see our ordinary world in a new and extraordinary way.

I began unschooling my children back in 2002 and that's what happened to me. My family was firmly ensconced in the ordinary world of school. My children were in grades four, two, and junior kindergarten when I first discovered the world of unschooling and chose to answer the call. When my children first left school, I had no idea what was in store for me—I just thought my kids were going to learn outside the classroom, and that was the end of the story.

I soon began participating in an online unschooling forum, then a couple of email lists, and then my learning began in earnest. I began questioning so many of my long-held assumptions about learning and parenting and children. No exaggeration, it was mind-blowing. And so began my inner journey.

I was active in online communities—as fit around our unschooling lives—and began a website to share information. In 2004, I wrote my first published magazine article about our experience and, in 2006, I began hosting a local unschooling conference and ran it for six years. I then decided to take that time and put it toward writing a book about what I'd learned through ten years of unschooling. I published *Free to Learn* in 2012. And I was still learning: I wrote on my blog, I wrote another book, *Free to Live*, and, in 2014, I became a regular contributor to the *Natural Parent Magazine*.

Meanwhile, I was introduced to Joseph Campbell's work and began to notice many subtle—and some not so subtle—connections between his monomyth and my journey as an unschooling parent. My curiosity grew, and, in 2015, I wrote a series of essays on my blog about my unschooling adventures through the lens of the hero's journey. Still, I couldn't shake my curiosity, and I dived into the idea of the hero's journey even more deeply, culminating in this book. And I'm still learning.

The quest that someone chooses to undertake that inspires them to question the conventional beliefs they've been handed about what it means to be human can be almost anything: Brené Brown is on a quest to understand humanity through the lens of courage and vulnerability, Amanda Palmer through the lens of music and art, and even Joseph Campbell through the lens of stories.

Our quest is unschooling.

TWO FUNDAMENTAL TRUTHS ABOUT UNSCHOOLING

Let's start at the beginning.

In our current culture, most people believe that learning of any value only happens in a classroom, with a curriculum, dispensed by teachers, and that children must be externally motivated to learn because it is hard work. Most of us grew up surrounded by these messages, and they've become part of our belief system about children and learning.

But you're here, and ready to question these assumptions. Maybe your first, fleeting glimpse of this other world—a world beyond schools, teachers, and curricula—came when you stumbled across a clue to one of these two fundamental truths about learning that lie at the root of unschooling.

The first truth is that human beings are innately curious, natural learners. To paraphrase John Holt (1983), an educator turned unschooling advocate: Fish swim, birds fly; humans think and learn. It's what we do. Watch a young child in action; see their enthusiasm to try things, before we start to pepper them with "No" and "Don't do that." When children are given the freedom to follow their intrinsic curiosity and explore the world around them with support from the adults in their lives, they learn. Full stop.

The second truth is that learning is everywhere. When we're playing a game. When we're at the store. When we're having a conversation. When we're watching TV. When we're out for a walk. Human beings are always absorbing information and weaving it into their understanding of the world, making it tighter and stronger.

These truths about learning lie outside conventional beliefs, which are wrapped up in the ordinary world of schools and gold stars. Choosing to accept this quest to create a thriving unschooling learning environment for your children is to embark on your own hero's journey to appreciate, understand, and, in the end, integrate, these unschooling truths—that learning is everywhere and that humans are wired to learn—into your lives. They will lead you not only to a new educational paradigm but also to a new perspective on day-to-day living. The rewards on this journey are amazing!

THE STAGES OF THE UNSCHOOLING JOURNEY

In this book, I'm going to walk with you through the stages of the unschooling journey, or, the hero's journey as seen through the lens of unschooling. Campbell structured his monomyth in seventeen stages, gathered into three distinct phases: departure, initiation, and return. As I dug deeper into the hero's journey from my unschooling perspective, I tweaked the stages to more directly reflect the landmarks and features common to the unschooling journey. Tweaking this mythic structure to the particulars of a specific journey is expected—that's why the hero has a thousand faces, after all. This table compares the stages and terminology we'll be using in this book with Campbell's original outline (Campbell 2008 28–29).

In the first phase, as we embark on the unschooling journey, we are likely to encounter various characters along the way: heralds that call us forward into this new world, guardians who believe they are protecting us by encouraging us to stay where we are, and guides who help us choose our next step. We'll grapple with our fears and uncertainty as we transition to a learning mindset—opening ourselves up in preparation for contemplating the many new ideas we will encounter on our journey.

Once we are packed and ready to go, the deschooling phase is home to our most intense learning. We will be challenging many of our conventional beliefs as we attempt to understand the nitty-gritty of how living and learning weave together. We'll reconsider the use of control as a parenting tool, and, in doing so, discover hidden depths of understanding—of both ourselves and others—that we may have only dreamt possible. We will tackle judgement, shame, and human nature, and come to find deep compassion in the sway of our days and with our children. Eventually, the ultimate goal of our quest is within our reach: unschooling with confidence and grace.

The third and final phase, living unschooling, explores our trek back to the ordinary world. We don't return empty-handed though; we bring our new-found wisdom with us, our elixir of life as Campbell describes it. Even so, this phase has its challenges. Our initial reception may be bumpy, and we may put off re-integrating for a while. In time, though, as we continue to pass back and forth between the two worlds—the conven-

COMPARISON OF JOURNEY STAGES

THE HERO WITH A THOUSAND FACES	THE UNSCHOOLING JOURNEY
DEPARTURE, SEPARATION	**CHOOSING UNSCHOOLING**
The Call to Adventure	The Call to Unschooling
Refusal of the Call	Refusing the Call
Supernatural Aid	Finding Our Guides
Crossing of the First Threshold	Crossing the Threshold to Unschooling
Belly of the Whale	Embracing Beginner's Mind
DESCENT, INITIATION, PENETRATION	**DESCHOOLING**
Road of Trials	Challenging Our Beliefs about Learning
	Shifting from Control to Connection
Meeting with the Goddess	Accepting the Value of All Experiences
Woman as Temptress	Accepting Our Nature
Atonement with the Father	Accepting Others Where They Are
Apotheosis	Cultivating Kindness and Compassion
The Ultimate Boon	Unschooling with Confidence and Grace
RETURN	**LIVING UNSCHOOLING**
Refusal of the Return	The Trek Back
The Magic Flight	
Rescue from Without	
Crossing of the Return Threshold	Crossing the Return Threshold
Master of Two Worlds	Being Ourselves in the World
Freedom to Live	The Flow of Our Unschooling Lives

tional world and the unschooling world—we begin to fully embrace our identity (our ability to be ourselves) in both worlds. We learn ways to flow more easily between them, coming to see how our two worlds are, in reality, one. Our world. This world.

Of course, there are infinite variations on these stages, hence the incredible range and depth of the world's stories—and the incredible variety among unschooling families. It will be helpful to remember that on our individual journeys there will be some stages you find more challenging, while other families seem to breeze through them. And conversely, there will be stages that you embrace quickly, but that other families struggle with. We all set out on our journey with our own unique set of experiences and assumptions that influence the questions we need to ask ourselves to unearth a bigger picture understanding of how humans learn, how we choose to relate to our children, and how to live curious and engaged lives in the world. All of which influences the twists and turns our individual paths will take.

There's an ancient Indian parable that illustrates this point beautifully, about the blind men and the elephant. A group of blind men try to learn what an elephant is like by touching one. Spread around the elephant, each of them touches a different part—a tusk, the tail, a leg, the trunk, an ear—and concludes from their singular experience what an elephant is like.

"It's like a spear!" "It's like a rope!" "It's like a pillar!" They proceed to argue long and loud about who is right.

We too may well begin our unschooling journey with certain beliefs and attitudes about learning, and see things solely from our perspective. This parable reminds us that what we are sure we know might only be the equivalent of the elephant's tusk. So, rather than gripping our viewpoint ever more tightly, we can choose to loosen our hold and consider the more unconventional ideas that will show up on our journey. Those other parts—tail and ear and trunk—might turn out to be integral parts of a bigger and more complete picture of learning.

A FIELD GUIDE FOR YOUR JOURNEY

Because each family's journey will be unique, I share this book as a field guide to the stages you are likely to encounter in some form on your unschooling journey. As I share snapshots from my experiences, know that they are not meant to be requisites. The stages of *your* journey may look similar, or they may look vastly different. Again, a thousand faces.

By getting a general sense of where we are in the monomyth's cycle, we can use the patterns to help us discover roadblocks on our journey. If you're having trouble starting out, why might you be refusing the call? If your overbearing aunt is upset with your chosen unschooling path, does placing her in the role of threshold guardian help you to have more compassion for her? Does it loosen the grip of the power she is trying to wield over you? On the road of trials, which pieces of conventional wisdom about learning or parenting might represent *your* most fierce monsters?

It's also helpful to note that, while I will be talking about many of the fundamental principles of unschooling, this book is focused on the journey and is necessarily more intuitive. It is a weave of stories, examples, and guideposts that have less of an intellectual basis and more a feeling of being lived and experienced. Unschooling is a mindset that bubbles up from within as much as it is a set of ideas to be comprehended and applied, precisely because of how well it aligns with the experience of being human. Sometimes it has more of a sense of "you'll know it when you see it." My hope is that the unique approach of this book takes the conversation around unschooling in new directions, helping you to learn as you go.

If you've yet to get a solid grounding in the basic ideas around unschooling, I think you'll find my books *What is Unschooling?* and *Free to Learn: Five Ideas for a Joyful Unschooling Life* helpful. You can find them, and others, on my website at livingjoyfully.ca/books.

And one last note. The self-awareness that arises as you read this book—thinking about the journey, while on the journey—may present some challenges. When laid out before you, it may be tempting to view the journey as something to be conquered, rather than explored and experienced. This perspective can bring out our competitive streak, challenging us to race through, checking off stage after stage. But to genuinely move beyond a stage, you need to not only understand it intellectually but also experienced it enough times in your lives that you deeply believe its truth.

How many times is enough times? I can't tell you that—it is unique to you and your journey. Also, don't be upset if you find yourself pulled back a stage or two, questioning things again that you thought you'd figured out. That too is part of the journey. The cyclical nature of life.

In *The Hero with a Thousand Faces*, Joseph Campbell writes, "we have not even to risk the adventure alone; for the heroes of all time have gone before us; the labyrinth is thoroughly known; we have only to follow the thread of the hero-path. And where we had thought to find an abomination, we shall find a god; where we had thought to slay another, we shall slay ourselves; where we had thought to travel outward, we shall come to the center of our own existence; where we had thought we would be alone, we shall be with all the world" (18).[1]

Welcome to the unschooling journey.

You are not alone.

1 From Joseph Campbell's *The Hero with a Thousand Faces*
   Copyright © Joseph Campbell Foundation (jcf.org) 2008. Used with permission.

CHOOSING
UNSCHOOLING

~ STAGE ONE ~

THE CALL TO UNSCHOOLING

YOU ARE THE HERO OF YOUR STORY.

Our journey begins in the ordinary world. What does that world look like to you?

For many of us, our worldview includes a pretty conventional perspective on education and learning. It goes something like this: we know that learning is the result of teaching and that school is where the trained teachers are, therefore, in order to learn, children need to go to school.

This is the narrative that most of us grew up with, and it's so deeply rooted in our society that we haven't seriously questioned it. Even if our own school experience was negative, we've absorbed the message that that was our fault. The idea that school is the best vehicle for learning is treated as fact, even though our compulsory education system has only been around since the early 1900s.

And then there's our current circumstances. Maybe our children are in school and we're dutifully keeping on top of their homework and test results, trying to help them to fit into the system. Maybe they're not yet school age, but we're concerned with school readiness; we don't want them to be behind before they even start. Or, maybe we're already homeschooling, yet still believing that the conventional model of teaching and curriculum is the only viable way for children to learn; we are implementing the system of school, but at home.

Regardless, we're established in our ordinary world and reasonably comfortable with how things are. We know the rules and expectations and, for the most part, we're happy to go with the flow.

But then, something happens.

CATCHING SIGHT OF OZ

Something gives us a glimpse of a new and previously unsuspected world: the world of unschooling. Maybe this first glimpse comes through the lens of school and learning, or parenting and relationships, or lifestyle and worldview. But the first pearl of conventional wisdom snags on the fabric of our reality, and things look different now. What had seemed acceptable before, now seems a bit less tolerable. We find ourselves asking questions that we hadn't seriously considered. What knowledge is valuable to an individual person? Can children learn what they need to know outside of school? Can learning really be fun? Now we're curious.

This is our call to unschooling.

In story terms, this call is typically delivered by a herald. It may be a person or an event, even an ordinary event, something that has happened many times before, but this time it leads us somewhere new. Often, it's not even something from the new world beckoning us in, but something—or someone—in our ordinary world who inadvertently says or does something that sparks a new level of awareness in us.

That's what happened in my case. The herald of my call to unschooling was the principal of the private school that my oldest son, Joseph, had been attending for a few months. We had a meeting to discuss how he was doing—I believe it was in January—and, armed with test results and some relevant articles from my education research to discuss, I was elated when the principal said, "We'll have to look for his gifts."

Finally, I thought. They are going to actually pay attention to him, to see him. But later that evening the real meaning behind that remark dawned on me: this environment, while better than the public school he had left behind, didn't allow him to thrive either. If it did, they would have already seen the engaged and interested (and interesting!) child that I saw regularly at home.

In my research leading up to that meeting, I had come across an article that mentioned homeschooling—I had never heard of it before. But just a few weeks after that meeting and the epiphany it sparked, I'd discovered that homeschooling was legal in Canada, that there were people actually doing it in my province of Ontario, and all three of my children had left school.

WHEN THE HERO IS READY, THE HERALD APPEARS

Campbell talks about the herald appearing when the hero is ready. The change that sparks the call happens within *us*. Even if we aren't consciously aware of it yet, we are ready for change and we begin to notice the signs around us. These signs are already there in our ordinary world—we are just now ready to see them. In fact, many of the stages on our journey will ask us to look more clearly beyond the conventional wisdom of our everyday world to see the clues that are already part of our lives, waiting for us to notice them.

These signs may include a growing discomfort with the institutional approach of the education system. Or recognizing that our child's needs are not being met in the classroom. Or maybe we hear about homeschooling or unschooling in a passing conversation and become fascinated with the idea.

And then the herald appears, often seemingly out of the blue. That person or event jostles the questions that have been bubbling beneath the surface, dislodging them, allowing them to rise to our consciousness. Now what? Are we going to acknowledge the questions and take this journey?

It may seem that our journey begins almost by accident, like the princess dropping her golden ball and it rolling into the water in the story of The Frog Prince. If we aren't ready to undertake the journey, these moments pass by almost unnoticed. The princess might have run home to get another ball, rather than being by the water when the frog appeared.

As for me, I could have chosen to wait a few months, hoping things would improve for Joseph, and scheduled yet another meeting with the principal.

And Theseus may have just accepted his father's burden—to send seven youths and seven maidens to be sacrificed to the Minotaur every seven years, as imposed by King Midas. This was his ordinary world. Instead, he volunteered to be one of the tributes and vowed to slay the Minotaur, or die trying. Theseus, though he did not know what he would find in the extraordinary world of the labyrinth, saw the call for tributes as his call to adventure. As things worked out, Ariadne, Minos' daughter, gave him a sword with which to battle the Minotaur and a clew—a ball of thread—with which to find his way out of the labyrinth. But he knew none of this when he first chose to answer the call.

Neither do we know much detail about what our unschooling world will look like. Yet, like Theseus, we get to choose our actions in response to the things we see around us. Which means, we need to be paying attention. These signs are not typically blinding, so are often not immediately understood.

We might hear of the strong and connected relationships that experienced unschoolers have with their children, and that seems impossibly delightful. We hear stories of the things they do, or don't do, and it seems almost unimaginable. But as we ponder them, as I did the real message behind the principal's remark, our curiosity about this strange, new unschooling world grows stronger.

Often, at the same time, the ordinary world one around us begins to feel strangely muted, and a bit uncomfortable. This call to unschooling signals a shift deep in our core, a chance to meet something "other," something bigger.

Are you ready to answer?

~ STAGE TWO ~

REFUSING THE CALL

IT'S YOUR CHOICE.

As much as we wish for smooth transitions in our lives, choosing to answer the call to unschooling isn't a simple question of yes or no and moving forward. As we begin to learn more about unschooling, life can sometimes feel like a see-saw. One day we're up, excited and imagining the possibilities. The next day we're down and fear looms large: we're stepping so blatantly outside the conventional education system. We waver. We wonder.

Will it really work out? If it's so wonderful, why isn't everybody doing it?

It's daunting.

Campbell describes this internal struggle as the choice between the comfort of the ordinary world and the imagined rewards beckoning from the uncharted one. It can be so tempting to stay wrapped in the warm blanket of our familiar lives, on our well-marked path. Change means opening ourselves up to the fear of not knowing what's ahead.

What dangers lurk there? Will these changes really be for the better?

These are good questions. Don't try to ignore them by turning up the excitement volume to drown them out. By exploring these kinds of questions as they arise, we discover the clear purpose and deep resolve that will help us on our journey. We need to explore our motivations and find our courage so that we can continue to move forward alongside our fear.

When you're feeling frazzled by the enormity of the journey you're considering, be careful not to berate yourself. Breathe. Take stock. The vast majority of questions spinning in your mind don't need to be answered in this moment. In fact, they can't be answered in this moment—it's a journey. Find a spot of joy. Even better, find that joy with your children. Take in this moment just as it is. Play. Start fresh. Again.

REFUSING THE CALL IS A VALID CHOICE

Refusing the call is a valid choice. There have been times when I discovered something new, enthusiastically dived in to learn more, then eventually decided it wasn't for me. This is me and vegetable gardening. I love the idea of growing some food in abundance and preserving what we don't eat for the fall and winter, and have been inspired a couple of times to give it a go. A few years ago, I even dug out a garden and planted for a couple of summers. I saw what other veggie gardens looked like, so I planted in rows for easier access, walked between the rows to discourage weeds, and one year I even managed to stake a few tomatoes.

But I soon discovered that I didn't have the drive to make the time to weed effectively, to learn more about how to care for the plants, or to preserve the bounty beyond what we ate. Instead, I gave some produce away to visitors who happened to show up at opportune times, and rationalized that the rest made great compost for the next year's garden. After a couple of seasons, I let the garden grow over—just keeping the plot was work I struggled to find time for. I heard the call and explored a bit, but found I didn't have the drive to follow through.

I could have continued to plant stuff, leaving them to sink or swim, and called it gardening. But I realized that left me frustrated and disappointed in myself. Why set myself up for that? Do the work or don't do the work. In the middle lies chaos, the seeming randomness of things gone awry more often than they needed, because I didn't know better. That frustration and disappointment, over and over. It can happen with unschooling too.

But let's face it, I can toss veggies in the compost and start over again, but we can't—or really, really shouldn't—keep going back to square one with children.

DON'T REFUSE TO DO THE WORK

Over the years, I've seen parents who answer the call to unschooling, yet don't follow that up with in-depth learning about how and why it works. They are looking for the reward at the end of the journey—the loving and connected unschooling family lifestyle they've read or heard about—without investing the time and effort required to truly get there. Without doing the work. They're looking for someone else to have done the work, an "expert," who will turn around and give them the answers. Just tell me what to do and I'll do it.

And that's understandable when we're first starting out—that's what learning looked like to most of us growing up. In school, the teacher was the expert and they had all the answers. We were expected to get the answers from the teacher or the textbook. That's how we were supposed to win the school game.

How could the unschool game be any different, in the grand scheme of things? It's just a different set of rules, right? A different way of learning, a different path to the same result: a competent adult. So sometimes, parents new to the idea of unschooling take the day-to-day actions of experienced unschooling parents and interpret them as a set of unschooling "rules" to follow.

No curriculum? Check. No rules? Check. Say yes? Check. Great! I can do this!

But real learning doesn't work this way. And neither does unschooling. As we touched on in the introduction, and as we'll see throughout this book, solid learning, learning that is understood and remembered, happens when we follow our curiosity, not someone else's rules. For our children, *and* for ourselves. For us to really begin to understand unschooling, we need to follow our curiosity and ask our own questions. And setting ourselves up to do just that is the goal of the choosing unschooling phase of the journey.

Let's go back to the vegetable garden analogy for a moment. Remember the chaos in the middle of trying to garden? I chose to move forward with a garden and made it look like a garden by following the rules I had seen around me, but I didn't follow through and learn any more. At the beginning of the growing season, it looked pretty damn good. Nice rows of plants, the odd weed only a half-inch tall. But a couple of months in and the garden was chaos. Rows barely distinguishable. Weeds competing full throttle with vegetable plants. Tomato plants bent over, brushing the ground. Monster zucchinis lurking under it all, growing wildly out of sight.

For parents who choose unschooling but don't dig beyond the rules, things can play out similarly. Their lives might look like unschooling for a while, but eventually they spin into chaos because they aren't building that long-term foundational layer of strong, connected, and trusting relationships that informs those seemingly relaxed unschooling choices and actions. No rules does *not* mean crazy free-for-all.

This too is a kind of refusal to take the journey. Or more precisely, it's like starting out on your journey, but then camping out at the first level spot you see and deciding to stay there. It might be nice for a while, but soon the animals will figure out where you store your food.

A lot of time and effort has gone into an experienced unschooling parent's ability to make their days look relatively easy. Or at least easy enough that others think all they need to do is imitate their actions and they're finished—they're unschooling. If you're going to start, take the whole journey so that you too can make your days look easy, though by that time you will understand, and deeply appreciate, the time and effort that has been invested in getting there.

ANSWERING THE CALL TO UNSCHOOLING

It's your choice whether or not to answer the call. Contemplating refusing the call shows that we are starting to understand the commitment involved in choosing to undertake the journey. Remember, refusing the call may just be part of your overall journey—if you choose to return to it.

In *Star Wars: A New Hope* (Lucas 1977), Luke Skywalker refused the call at first, citing his obligation to help his aunt and uncle, even though he dreamt of leaving. It wasn't until his aunt and uncle were killed that he answered the call to adventure.

Odysseus, happy in his ordinary world with his wife, Penelope, and young son, Telemachus, first refused the call to fulfill his pledge and recover Helen who had been taken to Troy. He even pretended to be mad, sowing salt in his field. To test Odysseus, Palamedes placed Telemachus in front of Odysseus's plow. Odysseus stopped and picked up his son, thus proving he wasn't mad, after which he could no longer refuse. He joined Menelaus's contingent, and launched the Trojan War.

The meeting that January to discuss my son wasn't my first meeting with the principal, but it was my last. And I may yet choose to commit to the time and effort of learning about and creating an awesome vegetable garden. Sometimes we need more time to prepare ourselves. But don't dilly-dally; with unschooling we don't get to start fresh every spring.

If you want to develop a thriving unschooling environment for your family, be sure to take the journey. Don't look for a shortcut. Engage with your questions as they arise, rather than pushing them away because they don't fit a preconceived idea you have about unschooling. This doesn't mean you need to understand everything about unschooling before getting started. It does mean that choosing unschooling with your family is the beginning of the journey, not the end.

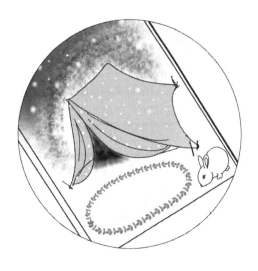

~ STAGE THREE ~

FINDING OUR GUIDES

THE WAY THROUGH OUR FEARS IS CONNECTING WITH OUR CHILDREN.

You've chosen to accept the call and embark on your unschooling adventure. At this point, your thoughts naturally turn to the road ahead. Fuelled with anticipation, you are more than ready to take your first steps. Sometimes, however, the questions and fears swirling through our minds threaten to overwhelm us.

How will I stay on the right path? Will there be clear signposts to guide me? What if I need help?

And, as with many tales, when we begin our journey in earnest a guide appears. Mythologically speaking, guides tend to be elderly—think Dumbledore and Obi-Wan Kenobi. But in a fun unschooling twist, I discovered the most important guides on my unschooling journey were my children.

The similarities between mentors and children as guides are interesting. Where elder guides have taken their hero's journey, travelling—physically or spiritually—beyond the ordinary world and returning to share their hard-earned wisdom, young children have yet to be acculturated. They still hold an open and curious view of the world, not yet having absorbed the messages meant to keep them safely in the metaphorical box of conventions.

John Holt describes the value of children as guides beautifully in his book, *Escape from Childhood* (2013): "Children tend to be, among other things, healthy, energetic, quick, vital, vivacious, enthusiastic, resourceful, intelligent, intense, passionate, hopeful, trustful, and forgiving-they get very angry but do not, like us, bear grudges for long. Above all, they have a great capacity for delight, joy, and sorrow. But we should not think of these qualities or virtues as "childish," the exclusive property of children. They are human qualities. We are wise to value them in people of all ages. When we think of these qualities as childish, belonging only to children, we invalidate them, make them seem things we should "outgrow" as we grow older. Thus we excuse ourselves for carelessly losing what we should have done our best to keep."

In my experience, a good portion of our unschooling journey is about excavating these long-buried traits—these human qualities—so we can once again enthusiastically engage with our lives. We rediscover our great capacity for delight, joy, and sorrow.

That said, let's talk about the idea of guide for a minute. There's a pretty common misconception that unschooling parents are following their children around, agreeing to their every whim. That's not what I mean by guides. Guides are not directors. Unschooling parents don't turn off their critical thinking skills nor do they ignore their hard-won life experience. No elder mentor asks that of their protegé either.

Yet, to develop the connected and trusting relationships with our children that allow unschooling to thrive, we don't treat them as the second-class citizens of the family. Their needs and wishes are as important as our own—our children aren't expected to fit into our lives. We weave a new life together, one that genuinely considers the needs and wishes of everyone in the family, regardless of age. We'll dive much deeper into this shift in the deschooling phase of our journey.

For now, it's enough to recognize that our children are shining examples of life outside our ordinary world, and they have helpful information to share with us. Hans Christian Andersen's fairy tale, The Emperor's New Clothes (first published in 1837), gives us a great example of a child as a guide.

~ ~ ~

There once was an Emperor who was so fond of new clothes that he spent all of his time and money on being well-dressed. One day, two swindlers came to the great city in which he lived and let it be known that they were weavers who could weave the most magnificent fabrics. And not only were their fabrics uncommonly fine, they explained, but they also had a wonderful way of becoming invisible to anyone who was unfit for his office, or who was unusually stupid. Word of this flowed through the city.

The Emperor paid them a large sum of money to start work for him at once. As the swindlers pretended to weave beautiful fabrics, trusted officials working for the Emperor visited to check on their progress. Imagine their surprise when they saw nothing on the looms! But determined not to let anyone think them fools, they praised the beautiful colours and patterns.

When the Emperor arrived to see the splendid cloth, he was shocked to realize he couldn't see the material. But to avoid being declared unfit, he too sung his praises at the empty loom. Nothing could make him say that he couldn't see anything.

At last, the swindlers declared the Emperor's new clothes were ready, and he arrived to be dressed. They made a big show of pretending to put the new garments on him, and the Emperor and his noblemen all spoke highly of the magnificent outfit. When it came time to leave, the noblemen pretended to lift his train and hold it high, none daring to admit they had nothing to hold.

The Emperor's procession got underway, and everyone in the streets and windows spoke of how fine his new clothes were. Nobody would confess that they couldn't see anything for fear of being declared a fool. The Emperor's new outfit was a complete success.

Then, in the crowd, a little child said, "But he hasn't got anything on."

One by one, people repeated in hushed tones what the child had said until the whole town cried, "But he hasn't got anything on!"

The Emperor suspected they were right but decided to walk on, more proudly than ever.

~ ~ ~

It took a child, not yet caught up in the cycle of judgment and shame of the Emperor's world, to speak the truth. Only once word began to spread did the adults find the safety in numbers they needed to say the truth out loud.

This isn't a recent phenomenon, either. I find it fascinating that Andersen was inspired by a similar story written by Don Juan Manuel and published hundreds of years earlier, in 1337, in a collection of stories titled *Count Lucanor* (Madsen 1999).

The story of the Emperor's New Clothes reminds us to listen to what our children have to say. Yes, they have less experience, but their perspective is less clouded as well. They often see things that we've discounted even before consciously considering them. On my unschooling journey, I soon came to appreciate my children's refreshing perspective.

Throughout this book, we'll be walking together through many of the fears that are likely to show up for you at various points on your journey. For now, I thought I'd share an example of how our children can be wonderful guides to help us move through them.

Sometimes my children became deeply engaged with a single interest for a long time. I began to worry, Were they closing themselves off, learning little about the world at large? Looking back, I could discern the pattern. One of them was superengaged with an interest over an extended period, and I was getting bored with it. I became less enthusiastic, which meant our conversations became shorter and shorter, until eventually, without my conscious realization, they pretty much stopped coming to share their new discoveries and insights. I figured I knew everything about the interest, so I stopped going to them to learn more. We drifted apart.

It was in those disconnected times that worry began to take root. With such a narrow focus, were they missing out on other great opportunities? Were they learning enough?

The first few times it happened, stressful days—and sometimes weeks—followed. I'd get stuck in my head, which led to even more disconnection and misunderstandings, fertilizing my growing worry. It became a downward spiral, and eventually, I'd end up asking myself why we started unschooling in the first place. Was this working? I wanted to show them the world! And they only seemed interested in a small pond. As I struggled with that question, I'd start imagining what days would look like if they went to school.

And it was then that I'd finally look at my kids again.

At first, I would imagine how much bigger their lives would be when they "had to" go out to school and do other things. Then I'd see them playing. They threw their whole hearts into it! I'd see them helping each other out. I'd see them persevere through a challenge. I'd notice how much progress they'd made in their video game since I'd pulled away. Or see their much-improved cartwheel. When they saw me more available—in mind, not just in body—they chatted with me more, and I heard shiny new words in their vocabulary. They asked me to play a new game or watch a new show or go for a hike. Days were fresh again. Soon I was actively engaged with them, and I saw their joy and their learning and their enthusiasm. They brought me back to what I already knew.

After a few of these cycles, I learned to recognize those worried thoughts more quickly when they started up (they are insidious—they often start to grow and fill us with unease before we figure out what's happening). And, rather than withdrawing into myself, I used them as a clue that it was time to stop ruminating and engage even more actively with my kids. My guides. To more clearly see them: their play, their choices, their actions, their words, their emotions. Even better, to shift directly into the moment and be with them. To sink into their play and absorb their joy and laughter.

And later, I would reflect. I would tease out the threads that wove through those moments. Those threads represent how our children see their lives and how they are putting the pieces of the world together. Their learning. Just when I thought they weren't learning anything new, there it was. It was there all along if only I had stayed engaged and connected enough with my kids to see it. The fear vanished. And every time that cycle happened, I built more trust in my children and in the process of unschooling.

Seeking guidance through observing and connecting with our children is helpful at all times, not just the challenging ones. It can be tempting to take advantage of times when things are going relatively smoothly to focus more on our own tasks. But in fact, this is a delightful time to check in, listen, and enjoy their presence.

And as you get in the habit of checking in with your children, you'll notice that sometimes when you thought things were going well, their actions or words seem to suggest otherwise. Be careful not to discount those messages just because you don't want to hear them. Your guides are warning you of real challenges to come if things stay as they are. Experienced unschoolers have discovered that subtle clues often show up before things get messy. It's better not to ignore them.

Another interesting tidbit: often the traits in our children that irk us turn out to be the precise ones that make them such excellent guides on our journey—our children challenge us in the areas where we still have a lot to learn. We're bothered by certain things because we haven't yet taken the time and effort to dig into them—if we had, we'd better understand our child's perspective, and their behaviour or choice probably wouldn't bother us even half as much.

And finally, if you're getting started on your unschooling journey and your children are just leaving school or curriculum-based homeschooling, they may have absorbed some conventional messages about learning. They may be tempted to agree that the Emperor's new clothes look rather splendid. For now, remember how free and happy they were during their last summer vacation, immersed in things they were interested in, engaged and learning like wildfire. That child is your guide.

Or, if your child seems to be a shadow of their former self, remember their engagement and joy with life before they went to school. Soon enough (on their timetable, not yours), they will rediscover their curiosity about the world around them, their love for games, or Lego, or stories. As they immerse themselves in fun, their love for learning will eventually re-ignite—they won't shy away from it. It's not important that they be able to name it, but that they are able to live it.

This focus on our children is not meant to discount the guidance we receive from more experienced mentors. The information and counsel offered by experienced unschoolers, both in person and online (or in this book!) can be invaluable on the journey. But in the end, this is your family's journey, so it's natural that your children are the most intimately involved. Not only are our children at the root of our motivation—the reason we began this journey to unschooling in the first place, but they are our most helpful guides when we feel we're losing our way. They are active participants in our days, mirroring our personal situation back to us to ponder. And, in the darkness, they are beacons of joy that are right in front of us.

Looking back, this shift to seeing my children as worthy guides on this journey was so valuable. When questions arose and fear-based "what ifs" began to swirl and surreptitiously pull me into myself, re-engaging and re-connecting with my children was invariably the best way to pull myself out of that downward spiral and regain my open, curious, and joyful mindset.

Our children will let us know if this is working well. Watch. Listen. Embrace life alongside them. That way you won't miss the clues.

Not for long, anyway.

CROSSING THE THRESHOLD TO UNSCHOOLING

MATCHING WITS WITH THE THRESHOLD GUARDIANS.

With your children by your side to guide you, you may now be ready to publicly declare your choice to step away from the conventional education system. You certainly don't need to shout it from the rooftops, but the people in your life will soon notice that your children aren't going to school.

In many myths, the hero—that's you—encounters one or more threshold guardians as they cross into the mysterious new world of their story. These guardians are often gatekeepers, like Cerberus, the three-headed dog of Greek mythology who stood guard at the entrance to the Underworld.

Some managed to make it past. Orpheus, a great musician, played his lyre so beautifully that he put Cerberus to sleep and entered the Underworld in an attempt to bring back his wife, Eurydice. Heracles' (aka Hercules) twelfth and final labour was to bring Cerberus to Eurystheus, the king of Mycenae.

Interestingly, looking back, I recall being challenged in three different ways as I attempted to cross the threshold into the world of unschooling. How fitting to envision each as one of Cerberus's three heads. This stage is all about figuring out how to move past these apparent gatekeepers and continue on our journey.

Let's go!

HEAD #1: TESTING OUR RESOLVE TO LEAVE THE ORDINARY WORLD

The first head represents the guardians of the ordinary world, intent on keeping people from leaving. Its growling and barking warn you not to wander too far away from the village, your ordinary world, where the conventional rules of parenting and education will keep your family ensconced, along with everyone else, in the day-to-day minutiae of community life.

What might that look like in our lives?

Often, it's family and friends pointedly questioning our choice to not send our children to school. Maybe they're urging us not to embark on this crazy quest. Their tactics can range from head shakes and eye rolls when homeschooling comes up in conversation to outright arguments, insisting that we're making a huge mistake.

These unofficial custodians of the established bounds of society believe they are acting in our best interests as they vigorously discourage us from entering the realm of unschooling. They want to protect us and our children. They are often people who care deeply about our family and feel a responsibility toward us.

Their sheer confidence can be daunting. Not only that, in a perverse twist, their warnings are usually not of mysterious monsters lurking in the dark world of unschooling waiting to pounce on us, but that we will be creating monsters *of our children*. They are certain that if we take our children on this journey, they will become uneducated, unsocialized, out-of-control adults—failures who will never be allowed back in the village, forever shunned.

We're pretty sure this will not be our children's fate, so, we might try to argue our way past these guardians. Maybe we're at a family get-together and the conversation goes something like this:

"Hey! I just heard your kids aren't going to school. Is that even legal here?"

"Yes, it's legal."

"Does the school give you the curriculum or do you have to buy one yourself?"

"Um, no, they don't give us a curriculum. I don't think we're going to use one, actually."

"What? How will you know what to teach them?"

"Well, I'm not going to sit them down and teach them. They'll learn whatever they want to learn."

"Whatever they want to learn? Kids don't want to learn. Just look around. You practically have to bribe kids to pay attention at school nowadays."

"Well, yeah, but when you let them play, they learn lots."

"Maybe, but that's not the important stuff. They're not going to learn how to read by playing. What about tests? They have to take some kind of standardized tests to show the school, right?"

"No. I mean, the kids can take them if we want them to, but I don't."

"Seriously? If you don't test them, how will you know they're even learning?"

"I'm with them every day. I can see that they're learning stuff."

"I couldn't imagine spending all day with my kids; I'd go crazy. What about math? You hate math, right?"

"Well, they'll learn math when they're cooking and stuff."

"Cooking?" They give you that are-you-serious look. "But they'll go to high school, right?"

"Maybe ... if they want to."

"If they want to? But they'll be missing out on so much fun with the other kids. And prom! High school was the best. And they'll never get a good job without a high school diploma. They'll end up flipping burgers their whole life."

Now, quick question. Whose voice did you hear in your head as you read that? Remember that for later.

When we first took the kids out of school, I had numerous versions of that conversation. The other person was sure I wasn't accepting reality; that I was living in some fantasy world where children love learning and jobs will fall into their laps. In turn, I would feel defensive and was sure they weren't seeing the real reality, where children hate learning and only go to college because they have to.

We weren't going to change each other's minds in that conversation; we were only going to become more entrenched in our positions. The thing was, I didn't yet understand unschooling well enough to be able to answer their concerns any more completely. And I didn't yet have my own children's unschooling experiences to share as examples. So, of course, we were stuck.

Around this time, I came across the pass-the-bean-dip suggestion. Experienced unschoolers reminded me that I didn't have to get pulled into those frustrating conversations. Instead of feeling the need to defend myself and getting caught in the inevitable downward spiral, I could politely answer that first question or two and then change the subject. "Pass the bean dip, please." "What have you been up to lately?" Or, "I'm going to go check on the kids," if you feel the need for a change of scenery. Even if the kids aren't there, there's always the plausible need for a bathroom break. It takes two people to continue a discussion, and *you are free to leave any time.*

As I began to navigate beyond my instinctive defensiveness, I also came to realize that, although I was super excited about our choice to unschool, I didn't need to make this a line in the sand with friends and family. For all the wonderful things that I anticipated would come from this journey, most had yet to materialize. Although I was beginning to understand unschooling, my understanding was still mostly theoretical—it wasn't yet supported by *my* personal experience. So, rather than endlessly trying to defend myself, I could instead truthfully say, "We're going to try this for now. It feels like a good fit for us. We'll see how it goes."

As it turns out, these threshold guardians serve a useful purpose: testing our resolve to undertake this journey. If we're going to give up as soon as someone questions us, we're in for a rough ride ahead. This won't be easy—it will take work. We are going against the grain.

What their objections often do is help us realize how dependent we are on their approval. That takes some personal work to get through, yet once we realize that we don't need to convince anyone to "let us" embark on our journey, we find ourselves free to go. Wow! We feel like we've released a ton of weight that we didn't even realize we were carrying. *We don't need their permission.* Cerberus's first head can bark all it wants, but it doesn't scare us anymore.

We remember, yet again, that it is our choice to forge ahead.

HEAD #2: TESTING OUR WORTHINESS TO ENTER THE NEW WORLD

The second head represents the guardians of the new world but, rather than trying to keep people from leaving, they seem to be trying to keep people from entering. See the difference?

What might that look like in our lives?

As we attempt to cross the threshold into the world of unschooling, it's not unusual for us to believe that what we're doing is choosing a different education path. I know that's where I started. My kids went to school to learn, and now they aren't going to go to school anymore, so this unschooling thing is a replacement for that classroom learning. I knew our lives would be different (I mean, the kids weren't going to school!), but I wasn't yet aware that this path was going to permeate all corners of our lives.

I didn't know anyone in person who was homeschooling, let alone unschooling, so I began to reach out and connect with experienced unschooling parents through the online community. I found most were welcoming and encouraging. There were times, though, when newer members posted questions, and the answers almost felt like personal attacks—especially online, where we can't read tone and body language. And sometimes those answers were interpreted as attempts to keep people out of the unschooling world.

"What do you mean, I'm not an unschooler if I don't?"

Fill in that blank with whatever belief you might be feeling unjustly challenged to confront at the moment. 'That's crazy!' you think. 'What does that have to do with unschooling anyway?' When I began reading online about some of the things unschooling families were up to, especially in the area of parenting, I remember thinking, 'Well, we won't be doing that.'

It's human nature to feel defensive when our beliefs are challenged—and just when we've risked so much to change our conventional beliefs about school! Maybe we're still smarting from having to defend our unschooling choice to family and friends as we confronted Cerberus's first head, and now we feel like we are being rejected by those in the new community we so excitedly want to join.

In those moments, I chose to notice my feelings and then release them. I was so curious! I hungrily absorbed all the unschooling information and discussions I came across. The information I was finding out about how humans learn aligned so closely with my personal experience and my observations of my own children's learning that I knew there was something to this unschooling thing and I was determined to learn more.

Spoiler alert: In a few months, I was doing many of those things I initially dismissed—they began to make sense as my understanding of unschooling grew. But let's not get too far ahead of ourselves.

After seeing this kind of interaction—this push and pull of determination and defensiveness—play out time and again over the years, I've come to see it as a pretty classic component of this stage. Eventually, the realization dawned on me that these threshold guardians were not enemies trying to keep us out—they were allies trying to help us learn.

Experienced unschooling parents encourage us to look at situations from new perspectives that are more conducive to unschooling. But it can be very unpleasant to have someone contradict the beliefs and assumptions that we hold as truths in our lives—beliefs that we don't yet realize are connected to this journey. It can be hard, personal work for us to shift from seeing them as attacking enemies to seeing them as allies providing us with useful information. I found it so valuable to develop the ability to use that initial defensive reaction as a clue to stop, breathe, and shift to an open and curious mindset.

Remember our discovery in the last stage, that the traits in our children that irk us are often great clues to where we have the most to learn? Same thing here. The more vehemently we resist an idea, the bigger the clue that there is some important learning for us buried there. If we are willing to dig deeper, there's probably a big jump in understanding around the corner.

What we learn as we confront Cerberus's second head is that not all guardians are meant to be defeated, some are really allies in disguise. There are many experienced unschooling parents who are happy to share solid information to help us on our journey. These challenging moments remind us that understanding unschooling takes real effort, and will likely be uncomfortable at times, but the wonderful stories that these very guardians share about life in this new world remind us that this journey is worth it.

We are getting stronger.

HEAD #3: SECURING PERMISSION TO HOMESCHOOL

The third head represents the official guardians tasked with giving travellers permission to cross this particular threshold. Most countries around the world have compulsory education laws of some sort and government representatives that require us to follow those laws. They are one of the more easily recognizable threshold guardians—almost like border guards, checking our papers. It can be tempting to approach these gatekeepers adversarially, but they too serve a useful purpose: to ensure we understand the legal implications of our choice to homeschool.

Notice that I use the term "homeschool." That's the typical term used by government education departments to describe students who don't attend school. Unschooling is a style of homeschooling, and there's no need to get that specific. In fact, with misconceptions about unschooling swirling around, using that term may hurt more than it helps.

Take some time to research your region's homeschooling policies, and determine what steps are required to legally homeschool your children. If the policies are fuzzy, or if there are reporting requirements you are unsure about, search out a local homeschooling or unschooling person or group. In my experience, they are happy to share how the policies play out in their unschooling lives. Remember, they are our allies.

That said, some families choose to unschool under the radar. That is, they don't engage at all with their government about the education of their children. This is certainly a choice, yet the step of researching your particular legalities is still important. It allows you to make an informed decision, which includes understanding the risks and implications to yourself and your children. Don't bury your head in the sand, ignoring reality. Whatever your choice, fully understanding the situation makes it an empowering one.

Whether you've chosen to complete the task set for you and submit your papers, or to walk past the gate while they're looking the other way, congratulations. You've made it past this more official guardian, the third of Cerberus's heads.

What an intense stage! And as we find our way around and through the various threshold guardians that appear on our path, maybe even making allies of some, the path on the other side of the threshold begins to come more clearly into focus. We catch longer glimpses of the wonderful unschooling world that beckons to us.

And we step across the threshold.

~ STAGE FIVE ~

EMBRACING BEGINNER'S MIND

TRANSITIONING TO A LEARNING MINDSET.

Here's how Joseph Campbell describes this stage: "The hero, instead of conquering or conciliating the power of the threshold, is swallowed into the unknown, and would appear to have died." [2]

My first thought was, "What?!" Don't we now find ourselves in this new and mysterious world of unschooling, excited to be on our way? We've worked so hard to answer this unconventional call, discover our guides, and make our way past the three heads of Cerberus that stood at the threshold, and now, apparently, we "appear to have died?"

What's up with that?

---

2   From Joseph Campbell's *The Hero with a Thousand Faces*
    Copyright © Joseph Campbell Foundation (jcf.org) 2008. Used with permission.

Interestingly, our journey has another surprise in store for us. There is one last important step the hero must take before they enter a new world, and that's transitioning to a learning mindset, otherwise known as beginner's mind.

LEAVING THE ORDINARY WORLD BEHIND

Right now, you probably believe that much of your existing knowledge about the ordinary world will be applicable—even helpful—on your journey. Spoiler alert: it won't. In fact, it's more likely to get in your way. On this unschooling journey, you will question so much of what you think you already know. If you don't first diligently widen your perspective, you may find yourself clinging to your existing paradigms, and feel the urge to defend them rather than being open to seeing the possibilities that this new world has to offer. You may have experienced some of those defensive feelings in the last stage.

As we begin this stage, for all our excitement about entering this new world, we're also still fearful of letting go of the old one. We want the two worlds to mesh. We seek out compromises. "But you still teach them to read, right?"

While I understand (and remember!) this wish to keep one foot in both worlds, it takes both our feet to keep moving forward. The first step is finding the courage to lift up that second foot and leave the ordinary world behind once and for all. It is our metaphorical point of no return, the last stage of the departure phase of our journey.

Being swallowed is a popular image in stories that symbolizes a transition. It describes the hero's figurative death in the ordinary world and their rebirth in the new one. Philosophically, it's about shedding our preconceptions (assumptions that made sense the ordinary world), and embracing beginner's mind (open to learning about the new world). Campbell calls this stage the "Belly of the Whale." It's an apt metaphor, and this whale comes in a thousand different shapes and sizes.

Of course, there's the classic biblical story of Jonah and the whale. Jonah, unwilling to carry out a task that God had set for him, refuses the call and makes a run for it, determined to stay in his ordinary world. He attempts to escape by setting sail on a ship, but he is eventually tossed into the sea where he is swallowed by a whale. There he reconsiders his actions and, after three days, is disgorged—reborn—committed to his new world of serving God.

In *The Matrix*, Neo wakes up in his battery pod after taking the red pill. His escape from this "womb" closely mimics a human baby's birth: it's Neo's rebirth into his new world outside the matrix.

In *Harry Potter and the Philosopher's Stone*, the role of the whale is played by the Hogwarts Express. Harry leaves his ordinary world via King's Cross station and the magical platform nine and three-quarters. On the train, he gets his first taste of magic and realizes that he, like us at this point on our journey, knows little about the new world he's hurtling toward. But he disembarks excited and ready to learn.

In *The Hunger Games*, a train also marks Katniss Everdeen's transition from her ordinary world, District 12, to the new world of the Capitol. She arrives determined to learn all she can so that she can survive the trials of the Hunger Games arena.

What might your whale be?

Like me, you may find that your whale is your home. I found that we spent a lot of time at home as we transitioned away from our ordinary world. Home felt like a sanctuary to all of us. For me, it was a place where I was free from judging eyes, at a time when I was most vulnerable to them. For my kids—turning ten, eight, and five that year—it was a place where they could dive into their play with abandon and make up for lost time.

We still occasionally went out to visit, but I found I had less and less to contribute to conversations with friends and acquaintances. I wasn't interested in converting friends to unschooling in any way, and though I was happy to answer any questions they had, those tapered off quickly as the conversation soon turned to the typical challenges of school and their children's behaviour. Those things were fast fading from my life, and I found that, with fewer and fewer things in common to connect over, we naturally connected less and less. I suppose that to our extended family and friends, we did "appear to have died," as Campbell describes.

But really, my family and I were happily cocooning deep in the belly of the whale: our basement. It was set up as a big playroom for the kids. Couches with removable pillows meant blanket forts for days on end. The walk-in closet under the stairs wasn't Harry's bedroom, but it was filled with shelves, which in turn were filled with games and toys. There was a large kid-height table for crafts and lots of floor space for play. A TV with game consoles. A computer with Internet access. An elaborate hamster city with cages, tunnels, and accessories. Lots of light. We spent months there, having a lot of fun!

It was natural for us to withdraw from the ordinary world, and it may be right for you as well. This time in the belly gives you the space to play with the idea that you may know little about this new world you are choosing to enter. As part of your metaphorical rebirth, you are learning to embrace the idea that we are the equivalent of young children in this new world.

But it can be hard to admit we don't know things. Most of us have probably grown up with the idea that, as adults—as parents—we are supposed to know all the answers, yet, here we are, back to feeling the vulnerability of a child. To live with this uncertainty is challenging. Definitely uncomfortable. But knowing that it's natural to withdraw from the ordinary world at this stage of our journey may help ease our discomfort.

EMBRACING BEGINNER'S MIND

During this time, I watched the kids rediscover the joyful abandon of playing to their heart's content. I also had time to reconnect with them, and to ponder how well the conventional wisdom about children and learning that I had absorbed over the years meshed with the increasingly beautiful scenes I was seeing play out in front of me. As the gap between the worlds widened even further, I eventually chose to pick up my other foot and take that last step. I realized I had so much to learn about this new world! And that no matter my standing in my old world, I was a baby when it came to unschooling. And I was smitten.

And why is this image of rebirth so helpful to us on our journey?

Because babies are the ultimate learners. Their drive to explore their world and learn how it works knows no bounds! Not only are they insatiably curious, they also aren't yet carrying the weight of conventional expectations. They look at the world with a beautiful sense of wonder. They live wholeheartedly, putting all their being into each moment—good and bad. And they aren't afraid to ask questions. Boy, do they ask a lot of questions!

It's important at this stage to make clear, unbiased observations rather than jump to judgement based on our old ways of seeing things. We will feel freer. With this fresh perspective, we begin to feel comfortable asking questions again, even if only of ourselves. The root of the word question is "quest," and we are on a quest to understand unschooling.

And remember, our children are our guides—our shining examples of how to do this, of how to re-engage our childlike curiosity and sense of wonder. It is important that, as we enter the unschooling world, we have a real sense of leaving our ordinary world behind, and understand that we are the equivalent of newborns in this new world. Embracing beginner's mind is the ultimate learning mindset.

UNSCHOOLING IN THE WILD: RULES VERSUS PRINCIPLES

As we consciously begin to approach our days with the fresh eyes and learning mindset of beginner's mind, we often encounter the unschooling idea of rules versus principles. Why do we focus on this distinction? Because when a rule is pulled out, everyone stops thinking and learning. Rules are quick answers to typical situations, which means that when we fall back on one, we consider neither the nuance of the particular moment, nor the current motivations and goals of the individual people involved. Where rules scream stop, principles ask for a pause.

Principles are a much more useful tool for learning about the real depth of a moment. They invite conversations, questions, analysis, openness, and creativity. These moments are great opportunities for our children to learn more about the world, about others, and about themselves. And it's in these moments that deeper understanding and trust take root. We begin to discover what works well for our family, because the path forward can be as individual as the people involved, and the circumstances of the moment.

In my experience, one of the common first responses to hearing this idea of moving away from rules is along the lines of, "That makes sense, but there are still some rules we need to keep, right? Like around safety?"

It sounds logical, doesn't it? But it's a clue the person still has one foot in the ordinary world. They are still holding onto the conventional wisdom that the only way to keep people safe is through rules. With both feet firmly planted in a beginner's mind perspective, the question becomes, "How do I keep my kids safe without insisting they follow my rules?"

The thing with rules is that they put the onus on the child to follow them—and then we judge the child "good" or "bad" depending on how well they follow those rules. But in this new world of unschooling, instead of putting the responsibility for avoiding those risks on my child by invoking a rule, I choose to take on that responsibility myself until they can safely take it on themselves.

Let's look at the ubiquitous childhood rule, "Don't go on the road." If we were in a situation where there was a chance my young child might inadvertently run onto the road without looking, I would stay with them. We'd chat about our environment, including the nearby road. If our play got close, I'd mention moving away a bit. If a ball rolled onto the road, I'd walk them through a safe way to retrieve it—a real reason to go on the road that the rule doesn't take into consideration.

That is how children (and adults) learn: through experience in their environment. They don't want to get hurt. What children need—and want—is to learn is how to evaluate the risk of being hurt in the different environments in which they may find themselves. So, you point out the nearby road, the hot stove, the long staircase, but if you don't think they are yet able to make safe choices for themselves, don't hand them that responsibility by passing on a rule and then blaming them if they don't follow it. And if they are able to make safe choices—which we eventually see through their actions—they don't need the rule. Again, they don't want to get hurt; it's not fun.

See how the rule gets in the way of their learning? If we share the rule, we stop there. We don't share the world of consideration and analysis that lies beneath it. And with unschooling, our goal isn't for our children to be able to recall a set of rules to follow but to be able to think for themselves. That way, when they come across a situation for which there wasn't a rule, they don't flounder, they figure it out.

Does that sound like it takes a lot of time to do? It does. And about now you may start to realize that by choosing to enter the world of unschooling, you now have this time available. Time to play with your children, time to chat with your children and hear what they're thinking, time to observe your children in action and see them making choices. Our presence replaces the need for rules.

FINDING ALLIES

As we cocoon in the belly of the whale—whatever that looks like for us—and embrace beginner's mind, the next question is often, "How can I learn more about unschooling?" Answering this question involves sorting through the potential sources of information. Unschooling has been growing in popularity, which means there are more and more people sharing their experience and insights online, and more and more local groups getting together for park days, field trips, and coffee chats. That means there's more choice. And that's wonderful! But it doesn't mean that all of them will be a good fit for you, or for your children.

It's like when my son Michael first wanted to try karate. We found a dojo relatively close, but before we went, I was careful to mention that if he didn't like it there, that might not mean that he doesn't like karate. It may just mean that he doesn't enjoy the atmosphere of that particular dojo, and if that happened, we could try another one.

Interestingly, over the years I've seen parents who don't quite connect with the dojo atmosphere go to Sensei and try to get him to change certain aspects so that it would be a better fit for them personally. However, the leader of any group activity has probably worked hard to cultivate the atmosphere they feel is best, the one they wanted to create. If it doesn't mesh well with you and your child, that doesn't mean it's wrong, only that it's wrong for you folks.

Same goes for online unschooling groups. Check out a bunch of them and see how they feel to you. How do you like to learn? You will learn more quickly if the group fits your learning style. Pay attention to the communication style of the more experienced participants, and be sure to check out the information they share. Is it making sense? Be careful though, don't equate meshing with a group to feeling comfortable. Unschooling is likely to challenge many of your core beliefs about learning and parenting—that will sometimes feel very UNcomfortable. You're not looking for a pat on the back; you're looking for solid information. Understand that that may very well stretch your comfort zones.

To that end, don't only focus on the flow of day-to-day conversation between members. Pay attention to the stories being shared by the more experienced members and their relationships with their children. Is that what you're striving for? It's not just about what to do today. The steps they are talking about will lead in that same direction. Is that the direction you want to be heading? By asking yourself these questions, what you're doing is building trust in the groups that you will choose as your go-to sources of information in this new unschooling world.

And when you find a handful of groups that seem to mesh well with you, dive deep. Continue to read—articles, books, online conversations. Read the responses to questions you hadn't even considered yet. To questions about children who are years older than yours. Or younger. Listen to podcasts and talks or watch videos—however you like to immerse yourself in information. Explore the ideas of unschooling in all sorts of circumstances, not just those applicable to your family today, because seeing how these principles are applied to many different situations will help you better understand them. Which means, as new-to-you situations come up over the years, you'll already have had lots of practice in seeing them through the lens of unschooling. You will learn so much more, and learn it more quickly, than if you just go to the group whenever you have a particular question or issue.

And it all starts with embracing beginner's mind. This stage marks our final separation from the ordinary world and our rebirth in the world of unschooling. We are truly open to new ideas, ready to question everything and face the trials of the next phase of our journey.

DESCHOOLING

CHALLENGING OUR BELIEFS ABOUT LEARNING

NURTURING THE JOY OF LEARNING.

We are in the world of unschooling now! With a clear choice to embrace unschooling, and our departure from the ordinary world complete, we find ourselves, in Campbell's parlance, in the initiation phase of our journey. In the unschooling world, this intense phase of our inner journey is often better known as deschooling, which means that over the next seven stages we are going to do an incredible amount of questioning, soul-searching, observing, thinking, learning, and growing.

On the hero's journey, the first stage of initiation is known as the road of trials—a series of tests and challenges that the hero faces as they begin this personal transformation in earnest. And we are in good company! Dorothy's trials in *The Wizard of Oz* were laid out for her along the yellow brick road. Through her quest to return home, she and her allies, the Scarecrow, the Lion, and the Tin Man, discovered that what they were seeking was inside them the whole time. Frodo Baggins, along with his trusty ally Samwise Gamgee, overcame a multitude of both physical and spiritual challenges on the road to Mordor in his quest to destroy the one ring. Hercules was given twelve labours to accomplish on his road to atonement.

On our unschooling journey, you too will undergo a personal transformation through the challenge to many of your existing beliefs. So many, in fact, that I've broken the road of trials into two stages: one around learning and the other around parenting. These are the areas in which you will face your most daunting tests. The order in which you tackle them isn't particularly important. You will probably want to focus first on whichever one called you to undertake this unschooling quest in the first place: discontent in either the area of learning or parenting. From there, one leads to the other.

Who knew learning and parenting were so inextricably linked?

Yet that's what you'll discover in these next two stages of your journey. So, let's get started!

Since I began my deschooling phase by exploring learning, we're going to start there. I'm going to share five unschooling truths about learning that may, at this point on your journey, seem a bit outlandish. Just begin wherever you are, with the openness of beginner's mind, and start asking yourself questions. Twist and turn each of these ideas around in your mind to see them from different angles. For example:

- How does the idea of unschooling fit with your experience with learning inside the school system?

    o Did you enjoy school? What classes did you like? Did you do well on tests? Were they an accurate reflection of your knowledge and understanding? How much do you remember from your various classes now? And after each answer, as yourself why or why not to dig deeper.

- What about your experience with learning outside school?

  - Your hobbies, jobs, personal projects—how have you learned new things since leaving school? Do you remember what you learned on your own more easily?

- How were the school experiences of your partner, family, and friends?

  - What's different between the people you know who enjoyed school and those who didn't? What impact has that had on their lives?

- How does it fit with the learning you're seeing with your children?

  - How did they learn in their early years—to walk and talk and eat— and at school, if they've been?

I suspect you'll move through some of these ideas relatively easily, while others will present more of a challenge, and you'll need some time and determination to find your way through. Either way, as you explore these principal truths about learning and contemplate the questions that come up for you, your understanding of the fundamentals of unschooling will grow.

TRUTH #1: TEACHING IS NOT A PREREQUISITE FOR LEARNING.

With unschooling, we make a clear distinction between learning and teaching. Real learning happens in the learner. That is, learning that is understood and remembered, versus memorized and soon forgotten. I imagine you remember times at school when your teacher stood at the front of the class teaching earnestly, and you didn't understand or weren't paying attention. No learning happened. And on the flip side, I bet you can recall learning things when you were all by yourself, just figuring things out. For learning to happen, teaching needn't be anywhere in sight. That said, as unschooling parents, we're happy to help our kids, to share our knowledge and experience anytime.

When a child (or adult) is pursuing something they are interested in, they are posing questions and exploring possible answers. What they discover through this experimentation often inspires new questions, with possibilities being tweaked and tried anew. That is the cycle of exploration and feedback, better known as learning. When things are interesting and challenging enough to keep us engaged and moving forward, but not so far over our heads as to completely stump us, we often find ourselves in our optimal learning zone—in the flow.

TRUTH #2: CURRICULUM IS UNNECESSARY.

With unschooling, we see the world as bigger and more diverse than a school's curriculum. But sometimes fears about leaving curriculum behind can bubble up. It feels like we're giving up the comfort and reassurance of having someone else tell us which of the many, many things in our big world are valuable for our children to know. Taking on that responsibility feels huge!

Then we take a deep breath. We remind ourselves that the unique set of knowledge and skills that will be valuable to an individual child will be different (maybe a bit, maybe wildly so) from the school's generalized curriculum. And then a refreshing realization hits us: what our child chooses to learn by following their curiosity and interests creates an individualized "curriculum" that fits them like a glove.

When I visualize learning, I see curriculum-based learning as linear, one grade to the next, each subject a separate line, insulated and unconnected. Life-based learning—unschooling learning—looks more like a web. Connections are made from one piece of information to another to another, following a child's unique path of curiosity, regardless of the subject or their age.

For example, an interest in baseball can lead to: math, as they analyze the batting and fielding statistics; geography, as they investigate the home countries of their favourite players; history and culture, as they learn about the ways the game has changed over the years; reading, as they devour websites and player biographies; health, as they challenge themselves to sprint the bases as quickly as possible; physics, as they try to consistently hit home runs; teamwork, as they try to work seamlessly together on the field; fair play, as they navigate the ups and downs of winning and losing; and so many other places! Because subjects in the real world are connected.

With unschooling, the process of learning looks the same for children and adults. It's how humans learn. Choice replaces coercion, leaving everyone free to learn, with the topic, style, pace, and depth under the control of the learner.

As people begin to release their hold on curriculum, the next question that often comes up is: "But aren't there certain things that a child has to learn? A base set of knowledge and skills that everyone needs to get along in our society?"

Sure, but unschooling children will learn those things precisely because they are living in the world every day. If it's something that's truly necessary to get along in their world, they'll come across a need to know it. Instead of seeing childhood as time spent being taught what they might need later, we see it as time spent living in the real world every day. When our children come across the need to know something, they learn it.

Not only that, learning is much more alive and engaging when a child is out and about in the world. It has so much more meaning to them because it bubbles up in real moments of their lives. The possibilities for learning when you're engaged in the world every day are more plentiful and more visceral than a classroom can ever mimic.

When we drop the assumption that learning only happens in a classroom, we begin to look for—and find—learning everywhere. And, tying it back to how this individualized "curriculum" fits unschooling children like a glove, it's reasonable to anticipate that the work and hobbies they'll choose to pursue as adults will be connected to their interests, so their unique set of knowledge and skills will be much more applicable to their future than a generalized curriculum. For example, Michael's interest in karate began when he was nine and continued to grow over the years, into acrobatics, then into performance martial arts, and now, as an adult, he's a stunt performer.

TRUTH #3: CHILDREN ARE ALWAYS LEARNING.

"Your job is to go to school and learn."

Did you hear that growing up? Maybe you've even said it to your kids. I probably said some version of that to mine when they were in school—it's a common analogy to make. But what it does is define learning as something that happens at school, full stop. So, by definition, what you do outside of school isn't learning.

With unschooling, we back up and realize that learning doesn't just happen in a classroom, with a teacher, during school hours. It can happen anytime, in any place, with anyone—or all alone. Not only that, unschooling is a learning lifestyle that never stops, there is no "graduation" from learning. There is no moment in time in which learning is "done." Lifelong learning—learning as children and adults—lives at the heart of un-schooling.

While we understand that the school system has a fixed time frame of compulsory school years within which they must move students through their set of curricula and be finished, we know that the timeline is arbitrary. There is no reason why a person can't learn about pioneer times or volcanoes at age seven, twelve, or twenty. When there's a need or interest, they learn it—their age is irrelevant. If they dive into volcanoes when they're twenty, that's great. There is no "behind" with unschooling. They weren't twiddling their thumbs when schooled kids were learning about volcanoes, they were learning something else in their world. Outside of school, a timetable for learning is irrelevant. We are always learning. We're learning with everything we do. It's time to expand our definition of learning to include all learning.

When we're talking about timetables and learning, one skill that often trips people up is reading. Conventional wisdom says that learning to read as early as possible is essential for children. Reading is a key skill in school because the entire teaching process is designed around it: textbooks, worksheets, tests, and so forth. So, not only are later readers shamed by being placed in remedial reading groups, their learning in all subjects suffers.

But when a child isn't in school, the necessity for reading so early falls away. Outside the classroom, there are many other ways to learn while they put together the reading puzzle: hands-on exploration, online videos, podcasts, audiobooks, documentaries and movies, not to mention a parent or sibling reading for them when the need arises. I saw this in action with my youngest. He was only at school for a half year of junior kindergarten, so, not yet reading or pressured to read in school. As a consequence, he learned to read in his own time. And, until he did learn to read, I got to see so many different ways of learning, sharing, and communicating in action. There was no hindrance to his learning at all.

It also helps that, with unschooling, the goal isn't "learning to read," it's pursuing their interests and passions. This gives them the space and time to explore the complex puzzle of reading without undue pressure or judgement as they chase the goals of their own choosing: like diving into a favourite world (with my daughter, the last pieces of the reading puzzle fell into place as she passionately explored the world of Harry Potter); texting with family and friends; playing video games on their own, and so forth. The possibilities are almost endless, and the paths to reading can be as unique as the individuals themselves.

Outside of school, there is no need to learn to read within anyone else's time frame.

TRUTH #4: LEARNING IS FUN.

How does your child like to learn? Schools promote and value the learning style that meshes with their process: a classroom with one teacher and many students. That's why reading and writing are highly valued.

With unschooling, a child is free to follow their curiosity in whatever way fits them and their circumstances, in that moment. Maybe they're watching a video about volcanoes for a while, then they want to make their own model so out comes the cardboard and paint, or the clay, and the baking soda and vinegar. Later that week at the library, they look for books about volcanoes to bring home. Maybe you point out some of the locations of active volcanoes on a world map, or a globe. Maybe you check out more pictures online, or more videos. Real learning is so much more interactive and fluid than a classroom can accommodate.

And again, the goal isn't the learning itself. When unschooling children are responding to their curiosity, following their interests and passions, and pursuing their goals, learning happens almost incidentally. But it's learning that makes sense and is remembered—it's real learning. And when they're doing that in the ways they enjoy, learning is fun! Even when it gets challenging because it's helping them accomplish the real things they want to do. Learning doesn't become something to avoid.

TRUTH #5: LEARNING IS NOT HARD.

Parents want their kids to think learning is fun with the hope that they'll want to learn, but when they go to school, what do the kids discover? That learning is hard. It's work. And, in those circumstances, from their perspective, it's true. Trying to learn something you're not interested in *is* hard. If the topic or information is unrelated to their lives, it often doesn't make sense; it doesn't expand their understanding of the world. In that case, they have to resort to memorization—it's just a piece of information floating around in their head, easy to forget after the test because they have no occasion to recall it. And with most of their time taken up with school, there's little left to pursue the things they do find interesting. As a result, their curiosity and drive to explore the world may fade. They just wait to be told what to do next.

Older students and graduates also often say they aren't creative. Sir Ken Robinson gave a great TED Talk about how schools kill creativity, explaining that young kids will take chances, be creative and original because they aren't afraid of being wrong, but that by the time they get to be adults, most kids have lost that capacity. "And we're now running national education systems where mistakes are the worst thing you can make. And the result is that we are educating people out of their creative capacities" (2006). Brené Brown (Kaufman, 2017) explains that "out of the many people that we've interviewed, 85 percent of them can remember something that happened in school that was so shaming it changed how they thought of themselves as learners. Of that 85 percent, 50 percent of those scars were specifically around art: writing, drawing, creativity, music." It's no wonder that once students graduate, many are loath to be proactive. They prefer to wait to be told what to do, in both work and personal situations, for fear of making mistakes.

But if you want to nurture your child's curiosity, cultivate their creativity and out-of-the-box thinking, and preserve their love of learning, unschooling is a great way to do that.

CHANGING HABITS TAKES TIME

What I discovered in this stage of the unschooling journey is that so much of the conventional wisdom around learning is intricately woven together with the needs of school. As you slowly but surely tease those threads apart, you can start to see what learning truly looks like, for children and adults alike.

And while you're exploring your beliefs about learning, don't forget to watch your children. Unschooling kids are wonderful examples of learning in action—that's one of the reasons they make such great guides! Be present and engaged with them, careful not to get caught up in your thoughts.

You may also find that you have other questions related to learning beyond the ones I've touched on. Great! Dig in and see where they are coming from. What messages have you absorbed about that aspect of learning? Do they align with your experience? What do you think the motivation was behind the messages? Ask experienced unschooling parents for their thoughts. How do their answers mesh with your experience?

As you explore this new world of unschooling and begin to uncover these truths, you are rewarded with new philosophical insights into learning. As a result, we often want to change some of our behaviour patterns—our actions and reactions—to better support our children. Sometimes it's relatively easy. But sometimes, even when we know we want to act differently, habit takes over and we can find ourselves playing out the same conventional scene over and over.

Shawn Coyne makes this astute observation in his book, *The Story Grid* (2015): "When human beings are faced with chaotic circumstances, our impulse is to stay safe by doing what we've always done before. To change our course of action seems far riskier than to keep on keeping on."

Change can definitely be hard. It can seem risky. But rather than being hard on yourself, just keep at it. Try to mindfully pause between action and reaction. Find yourself a moment of choice where before there was only thoughtless habit. Without the pressure of a schedule, there is time. Things don't have to move so fast.

And aim for small, realistic steps. Chaos and overwhelm is more likely when we try to make a bunch of changes in one leap. Try a little something and see what happens. If it works out pretty well, create yourself a reminder to try it again next time, maybe tweak your behaviour based on what you learned. Eventually, after enough repetition, you'll have developed a new habit.

It can't be said too often: we're always learning.

SHIFTING FROM CONTROL TO CONNECTION

MOVING AWAY FROM PARENTS VERSUS CHILDREN.

Now that we've explored the main conventional learning paradigms, in this stage, we're going to explore some truths about parenting. Does the conventional parenting wisdom that we're surrounded by really make sense? To explore this question, we'll be digging into our assumptions and expectations to see how well they mesh with our experiences, as well as observing how this new way of living—not going to school—is unfolding with our children. Our guides.

It's helpful to note that these ideas about parenting aren't exclusive to unschooling—you will see similar ideas discussed in attachment parenting circles, in consensual living groups, and even in traditionally published books about parenting such as *The Gardener and the Carpenter: What the New Science of Child Development Tells Us About the Relationship Between Parents and Children*, by Alison Gopnik (2016), a professor of psychology and internationally recognized leader in the study of children's learning and development. Her book is an interesting comparison of parenting metaphors. The gardener parent cultivates a rich and nurturing environment while giving their children space to grow into the individual they are meant to be (no two flowers are exactly alike), while the carpenter parent has a blueprint for the adult they want their child to become and diligently works over the years to ensure their child turns out according to plan. Gopnik argues that the carpenter approach, which has risen in prominence over the last few decades, becomes a toxic soup of expectations, anxiety, guilt, and frustration that has arguably made the lives of both children and parents worse. She concludes,

> Part of the pathos, but also the moral depth, of being a parent is that a good parent creates an adult who can make his own choices, even disastrous choices. A secure, stable childhood allows children to explore, to try entirely new ways of living and being, to take risks. And risks aren't risks unless they can come out badly. If there isn't some chance that our children will fail as adults, then we haven't succeeded as parents. But it's also true that being a good parent allows children to succeed in ways that we could never have predicted or imagined shaping.

Similarly, the parenting truths that are so valuable for unschooling to thrive are those that see the child as an individual in their own right. Moving away from the control tactics (the carpenter approach, in which the parent attempts to shape a "perfect" child) and toward the rich soil of connection nourishes a trusting relationship between parent and child. Between two human beings.

TRUTH #1: PARENTING IS NOT ADULTS VERSUS CHILDREN.

The presumption of parental power over children is so widespread in our culture that we often don't even think to question it. Well, now is the time. If you're feeling resistance to that idea, remember a couple of stages ago when we talked about embracing the openness of beginner's mind? Take a few deep breaths.

Power struggles between parents and children come about when parents insist and their children resist. It becomes a battle of wills, something beyond whatever the original issue was. When power is part of a relationship, everyone has to be on their guard, always, protecting the power they have by resisting advances and overpowering others when possible to gain more power. It's a draining and stressful way to live.

What if we drop the adults versus children approach to family relationships? What if we choose to help our children accomplish whatever they're trying to do? Help them follow their curiosity and explore the world for themselves? When everyone is pulling toward the same goal, there's so much less struggle.

Let's draw a parallel with our earlier rules versus principles discussion where we explored how principles open up discussion and help our children learn more deeply about the world than just following rules. When we're talking about relationships, focusing on connection also opens up discussion and helps children learn more deeply about their inner world (their goals and aspirations, their strengths and weaknesses—essentially, how they tick) rather than being told what to do.

Power struggles are not inevitable; they are a choice. Parents can choose not to engage in them. They can choose to treat their children like real people.

TRUTH #2: CHILDREN ARE CAPABLE OF MAKING CHOICES.

Conventionally, many parents make most of their children's decisions for them, believing they are modelling the "right" thing to do, and expecting their children to make the same choices when they are finally in control of their lives. This is more of the carpentry approach, often done more vigorously in the teen years.

Instead, rather than trying to teach your children the "right" choices to make, you can focus on helping them gain experience with making informed choices. Meaning, the choices that are right for them—in that situation, at that time. You can help them to brainstorm possibilities, discuss the pros and cons, and support them as they choose what seems to be the best fit for them. They will learn so much through the experience—and they'll see how their choice plays out so they can incorporate what they learn the next time a similar situation arises. Their self-awareness grows alongside their skill in making choices.

What we discover aligns with Gopnik's observations. When we aren't struggling with our children, but are actively nurturing a secure and supportive environment, children feel more comfortable exploring their world, trying new ways of living and being. This comes with some risk that things won't always work out, but that's the beauty of being free to make choices and learn from them. What we have discovered is that our children choose paths and succeed in ways we could never have foreseen.

One of the tips that helped me a lot when I was deschooling was, when my child asked to do something, to ask myself, "Why not yes?" So often we give a knee-jerk "no" as an answer. We're too tired, or it's too messy, or too dangerous, or too whatever. Is that really true? Or is it mostly an excuse? I found that when I stopped making excuses, I started living more fully with my children than I thought was possible. When I stopped trying to control most everything they did, our connection blossomed, and I saw how much sense their choices made. Children are incredibly capable.

TRUTH #3: FAIR DOESN'T MEAN EQUAL.

To be fair means to be free from bias. To not show favour to one child over another. We want all our children to feel equally loved, which conventional parenting wisdom has extrapolated to treating our children equally. It makes sense on the surface, doesn't it? To be fair, everyone gets one piece of cake—and you take care to make sure they're the same size. You spend the same amount on their birthday gifts throughout the year. They can each sign up for one recreational class or sport.

The challenge is that this looks at the situation from the outside, quantitatively measuring the facts of the situation, rather than taking into account the individuality—the unique needs, wants, and goals—of those involved. When we look at situations from our children's perspectives, things can look very different.

For example, imagine two of your children running up to you, both wanting you to come and play with them right now. Wanting to be fair, and knowing you need to do something in an hour, you may be tempted to say, "I can play with each of you for thirty minutes. We'll put on a timer to make sure you both get your time."

What if, instead of imposing your fair and reasonable-sounding solution, you chat with them and see what lies beneath their request? You may discover that your daughter wants to show you a ten-minute video she just found, and she wants to show it to you right away, while your son wants to play a board game, which usually takes forty-five minutes to an hour. As you discover this, you ask your son if he's okay with starting the game in ten minutes—he can go and get the board set up. He's good with that.

Ten minutes with your daughter and the rest of the hour with your son, and both children feel heard, respected, and have their needs met. They are equally happy. So often what seems fair on the surface may end up not satisfying the needs of anybody involved. Fair is everyone feeling that their needs and wishes have been heard, considered, and accommodated wherever possible.

As parents move to unschooling, they begin to see fairness not as a quantitative measure of what the parents give, but as a qualitative measure of the value each child receives. Again, as with learning, looking at things from their children's perspective. One child may need more of their parent's time, wanting a lot of personal interaction and attention. Another might have a passionate outside interest that needs more of the family's money to support it. Still another might need more of their parent's participation, actively engaging in their interests alongside them.

We may be giving each of our children very different things that take varying amounts of time and effort and money. But when their unique needs are met, they each feel content, secure, and happy: equally loved.

TRUTH #4: QUITTING IS NOT A FAILURE.

Choosing to quit an activity is as much a learning experience as starting it. Conventional wisdom says that quitting is akin to failure. That if children quit whenever they want, they will never finish something when the going gets tough.

One of the wonderful things about unschooling is that our children have time to explore the world, including a wide variety of interests and activities. But if we continue to insist that they finish what they start, they won't be learning the perseverance that we're probably hoping to instill. Rather, they will likely be learning not to try out new activities unless they are very sure they will enjoy it: the fear of being stuck in something it turns out they don't like will outweigh their curiosity to explore something new. That means less exploration and learning.

When we favour connection over control, our children gain lots of experience with wanting to try something, choosing ways to try it out, and seeing how well those paths meet their goals. They will discover things they enjoy and things they don't, and get a better feel for the clues that help them decide when to step up their game and when to quit and move on. They gain priceless life experience.

And each time they choose to quit, they're still learning so much. How does that choice feel? Do they miss the activity? If yes, what do they miss about it? What are they doing with the time that quitting freed up? Are they enjoying that? More? Less? So much learning.

Children who have the freedom to explore a variety of things and discard those that don't catch their prolonged interest do not feel like failures when they choose to drop something—they feel empowered. They see it as another experience from which they learned a little bit about something and a lot about themselves. And our support of their decision is a visible display of our trust in them to know what they need and want in that moment. They also know they can change their mind in the future—their choices are under their control.

Starting and quitting things, whether personal or organized, is about exploring their world—finding the activities and environments that spark their curiosity and bring them joy. If they discover a passionate interest, they will doggedly pursue it, even through many challenging moments. As parents, we don't need to teach this kind of unwavering commitment by requiring it in everything they choose to try. Instead, we can help them find things that they enjoy so much that their fierce dedication flows naturally.

TRUTH #5: STRONG RELATIONSHIPS ARE KEY.

Strong relationships are connected and trusting. I love what David Howe has to say about the value of relationships in our lives in his book, *Attachment across the Lifecourse: A Brief Introduction* (2011).

> Intimate attachments to other human beings are the hub around which a person's life revolves, not only when he is an infant or toddler or a child but throughout his adolescence and his years of maturity as well, and on into old age. From these intimate attachments, a person draws his strength and enjoyment in life and, through what he contributes, he gives strength and enjoyment to others. These are matters about which current science and traditional wisdom are one.

He concludes that sensitively responsive parents who can see the world from their child's point of view are likely to have securely attached children who, in turn, are most likely to develop emotional intelligence, good social skills, and robust mental health.

Rather than being entrenched in the parent-child power dynamic, parents can be in relationship *with* their children. When they are younger, we are their sturdy set of hands as they communicate their needs through cries and gestures: changing their diaper, feeding them, or bringing them a wanted toy. As they get older we slowly also become their sounding board and trusted confidant. Unschooling parents have discovered that connected and trusting relationships with our children are fundamental to allow unschooling to thrive. It is important that both children and parents feel comfortable approaching each other with questions and sharing their thoughts and feelings, without fear, and knowing that they will be heard. This is the safe and trusting atmosphere in which learning, love, and connection thrive.

Being able to see things from our child's point of view is crucial for helping them sort through situations and possibilities as they explore the world. Beyond putting ourselves in their shoes—what we think we would do if we were in their situation—because that's us looking at their situation from *our* perspective, with *our* experience, we put ourselves in their mind and body, seeing the situation through the lens of *their* experiences, needs, and goals. It's there that we can meet them where they are and connect intimately. And help them explore the possibilities for moving forward through the situation. The difference between sympathy and empathy.

The strong—connected, trusting, and respectful—relationships that we develop with our children will last a lifetime, not just childhood.

DON'T RUSH

I want to encourage you to give yourself time to ponder these truths. To see what they look like through the lens of your lives. As we talked about earlier, if you try to race through this, you'll miss so much of the value of the journey.

As Dorothy discovered in Oz, so often the answer we seek is right there within us; it only needs to be unearthed. That makes sense on our unschooling journey—it's not a quest that takes us to a literal new world, it's an inner journey of self-discovery. Some of the questions that crop up in our daily unschooling lives are almost expected, while others come out of left field. Sometimes we're thoroughly energized, and other times we're so exhausted that we're brought to tears, wondering where we'll find the strength to take another step.

When you're feeling overwhelmed, it's important to take a moment to clear the mental clutter and refocus. Breathe. Drink water. Sleep. Look to your children—your guides. How are they doing? That is our most important focus. If you've inadvertently pulled away a bit, this a great reminder to turn our energy back to them to make sure they are doing well. You may even find yourself re-energizing through them. I know I did. They are a boundless source of energy and joy!

Another deschooling tip: take note of those moments with your children when you see them shining brilliantly. In scribbled words before bed, or quick photos of the moment, or vivid memories etched into your brains. These snapshots will help to build trust in the process and can be a welcome ray of light during the more challenging trials.

On your deschooling road, you will discover things about yourself you didn't before imagine: the depth of your inner strength, the abundance of your love, and what you can learn by greeting your fears rather than running away from them. It can be exhilarating and energizing, yet racing down the road risks skimming the surface, short-changing this transformative process. It needs to take place in the roots of your being. Beyond what you are doing, into why you are choosing to do those things.

So be careful not to rush your learning. You will see people further on the journey and wish you were there. You'll get there—be patient with yourself. Yet, don't use that as an excuse to linger. Take it slowly, but surely. Keep questioning. Keep observing your children. Keep playing with your children. Play is important learning—for parents too.

There will be uncomfortable times. If you've taken a turn and there's no clear path ahead, practice sitting with the discomfort for a while. New insights and ideas can bubble up, answers may be unearthed, but only if you're patient and open to them—that beginner's mindset. Maybe you'll find your path just behind the tree you're resting against.

And remember, no matter how long you've been unschooling, as your children get older you will encounter new situations that you haven't yet worked through (at least not beyond the conventional response). Even those of us who have been unschooling for years can find ourselves off-kilter. We are always learning and growing.

ACCEPTING THE VALUE OF ALL EXPERIENCES

MOVING BEYOND JUDGEMENT.

Over the last two stages, you've confronted a lot of conventional wisdom around learning and parenting. You've worked to replace school and curriculum-based learning with learning through living—helping your children follow their curiosity and engage in their interests and passions. You've also taken great strides in replacing control with connection in your relationships with your children, taking each moment as it comes and working together to find a path forward that meshes reasonably well with everyone involved.

And you've started to see some of the beautiful ways in which these truths play out with your children. I bet there have been moments when you were amazed by their insight and choices! And times when you played with your discomfort to learn more about it. Your trust in the process of unschooling is growing as you add your personal experience to the mix, stirring it in with your initial intellectual understanding. And you've gained some well-earned confidence through navigating the twists and turns of the journey so far.

You can think of your deschooling story to this point as working through much of the nuts and bolts of unschooling, the hands-on details of living unschooling day-to-day. You see your children actively learning without curriculum or formal instruction, following their curiosity and flowing from one activity to the next, sometimes quickly, sometimes spending an extended amount of time focused on one thing in particular. Saying yes comes more easily to you. As does taking the time to solicit your children's perspectives, bringing their needs and wishes more thoughtfully into the conversation.

Now things get really interesting! As our understanding of our new world of unschooling grows, we are naturally drawn to digging deeper. I say naturally because, as I mentioned back in the introduction, our journey turns out to be about so much more than unschooling. We are exploring what it means to be a human being living fully in the world—in this case, through the lens of unschooling. Campbell's journey framework is descriptive, not prescriptive. Meaning, he looked at a wide range of stories and deduced their commonalities rather than coming up with the journey first and trying to find stories that fit. These patterns are how human beings are wired. I love how Jonathan Gottschall describes it in his book, *The Storytelling Animal* (2012): "If you haven't noticed this before, don't despair: story is for a human as water is for a fish—all-encompassing and not quite palpable."

THE UNIVERSAL MOTHER

Campbell calls this stage of our story "The Meeting with the Goddess." In myths and stories, the hero must be spiritually prepared to meet this revered goddess, the Universal Mother, who represents the whole cycle of life. If not yet ready, the hero is only able to see aspects of her. To meet her in her true form is to rise to her challenge and be able to contemplate the entire birth–death cycle she represents with equanimity. The ups and downs. The good and the bad. Cosmic creation and destruction. To be able to hold both these seemingly opposing ideas in your mind with comparable appreciation.

Kali, from Hindu mythology, is a great example of the kind of goddess you meet in this stage. As the goddess of time, creation, and destruction, she represents both the benevolence of a caring, comforting mother and the fury of an aggressive, punishing one, as well as the expanse of time that contains them both. You've probably heard the adage, "Change is the only constant in life." Well, Kali's four arms represent the rhythm of this change: creation and destruction, birth and death, good and bad. Typically, her two left hands hold a bloody sword and a severed head, while her two right hands depict protection and compassion. When we look at Kali's right side we see good; when looking at her left, we see bad. If we aren't yet ready to see her in her true form, we see one side or the other. But when we are ready to grasp the truth that lies at the heart of this stage, we see her full nature.

~ ~ ~

According to Hindu myth, Raktabija, whose name means "the seed of blood," was a demon who received a boon, or blessing, from Brahma, the creator God, that meant every time a drop of his blood touched the ground, a duplicate of himself would be created. Raktabija was a fearsome demon, causing a lot of trouble for both people and gods, but every time the gods tried to vanquish him, the battlefield became littered with his clones.

In desperation, the gods approached Shiva, one of the three gods responsible for the creation, upkeep and destruction of the world, but he was deep in meditation, and they were loath to disturb him. They turned to Parvati, his wife, and asked for her help in defeating the demon Raktabija.

Parvati agreed and assumed the form of Goddess Kali to do battle. Kali was fierce, with sharp teeth and wild hair. When she appeared on the battlefield, she struck fear into Raktabija for the first time. Understanding his advantage, Kali told the gods to attack the demon and then spread her tongue to cover the whole battlefield so that not one drop of his blood touched the ground. Unable to reproduce, Raktabija was finally vanquished by the gods. (In another version of the story, it was Kali herself who cut off his head and drank all of his blood.)

Having consumed all of Raktabija's blood, Kali transformed into a destructive force herself, killing anyone who crossed her path and decorating herself with trophies of battle: the heads and limbs of her victims. The gods, frightened and unable to calm her, decided to arouse Shiva from his meditation and asked him to intervene. Shiva found Kali and threw himself at her feet, which eventually calmed her, and she embraced him, shedding her deadly form.

~ ~ ~

This story is just one of the creation myths that surround Kali. We see how she came into being, with Pavarti transforming into Kali to help the gods defeat the demon Raktabija. Seeing a way to outwit the demon's trick, Kali saves the day by drinking all of his spilled blood so he may be defeated, but, as a result, transforms into a destructive force, killing anyone who crosses her path. Eventually, her husband, Shiva, is able to calm her down and she transforms into a gentler form. In her story, we see the cycle of creation, destruction, and back again, in the fullness of time. In fact, Kali is the feminine word for time in Sanskrit; she is the personification of time in Hindu mythology.

It's a captivating story, but how does it relate to our unschooling journey?

PREPARING TO MEET OUR KALI

All that we've learned on our journey so far about the world of unschooling has prepared us for this stage. We've been living our unschooling truths about learning and parenting for a while now. We've seen them play out in our lives, with our children, and we have some real experience under our belt. As insatiably curious human beings, we continue to ask ourselves why. As we continue to dig into these truths to better understand them, we soon catch a glimpse of what lies beneath. We start to see the connections between our unschooling perspective on why quitting things is not "bad," and why saying yes more is not "bad," and why our children seemingly doing nothing is not "bad." We notice that when we didn't stop our children because we feared they were making a "bad" choice, most often they went on to happily engage in the activity, see how it played out, and incorporate that experience next time. In other words, we saw them learning. A lot.

By giving our days the time to unfold more naturally, we've seen new and interesting things take root in the wake of destruction and upset many times. From a fallen block tower springs a taller and sturdier one. From highly anticipated plans falling through emerges a spontaneous trip to the park, or a cuddly movie day, which turns out to be just what was needed. Without knowing it, we have been thoroughly preparing ourselves for this meeting.

MOVING BEYOND GOOD AND BAD

Over time, we find ourselves no longer getting so angry when things to go badly. Experience tells us that something new and interesting may soon evolve to take its place. "When one door closes, another opens; but we often look so long and so regretfully upon the closed door that we do not see the one which has opened for us." This quote is commonly attributed to Alexander Graham Bell, and it succinctly describes life before this encounter with the goddess: we don't realize the connection between destruction and creation, between good and bad on the continuum of time. This is the wisdom that the stories of Kali and other Cosmic Mother goddesses are meant to convey to us on our life journey. Rather than being tossed around by the ups and downs of life, we now see the value of, and connection between, those moments. We have opened ourselves up to the bigger picture of life and the cosmos. And we're learning this indispensable aspect of being human through our unschooling journey. How cool is that?

So, we have been unschooling long enough now that we recognize the connections between the ups and downs of life and we've come to understand that we gain valuable insights into both kinds of moments. We know that, eventually, ups will follow downs. And vice versa. We've also experienced the cycle enough times to learn that trying to rush through the down times doesn't work—we can't pry open a door that doesn't want to give. That doesn't mean passively sitting back and waiting, though. In that case, you're likely to miss seeing the door down the hall swing open. Be attentive. Maybe knock on a door or two. Or three. Wander up and down the hallway so you notice if one's ajar. Listen, in case you hear the click of a door being unlocked. Eventually, something happens and things move forward, maybe in unexpected ways. And often in more interesting ways than we had imagined. That small, beaten up-looking door at the far end of the hall may open up to possibilities that fit you like a glove!

And this applies to our children as well. In fact, I distinctly remember that I first started making these connections in relation to my children's lives, not my own. Each time I chose to stretch my comfort zones and follow them where they were eager to go, I saw them learning so much, not only about the situation but also about themselves.

Both when things went well and when they didn't. Their self-awareness soared. I was humbled, seeing that my initial predictions—which I mostly kept to myself—were often enough flat out wrong. Without me clouding their experience with judgement, they could more clearly and directly learn what was most valuable to them in the moment. As my wish to understand my children's perspective and choices grew, my need to judge them faded away. With it, so did most of our conflicts. Our trust in each other grew.

It's important to remember, though, that not judging isn't about giving in or giving up. Or about saying, "Do whatever you want." It's about engaging even more deeply, but with the openness of beginner's mind. What can I learn here? It's about seeing the value of all aspects of life, moving through the "bad" moments with as much awareness as the "good" moments; not covering your eyes and trying to ignore them until they pass. All moments are an integral part of our lives, and they are most valuable when we're paying attention and learning what we can from them.

THE EPIPHANY

Earlier in your journey, you may have heard people in unschooling circles talk about how judging things as "good" or "bad" gets in the way of not only your children's learning but in developing strong and trusting relationships with them. I imagine it made some sense on an intuitive level, but mostly it was just another piece of the puzzle floating around in your mind. And, as you begin this stage, you may not yet have enough puzzle pieces to grasp what this "not judging" thing might look like in the bigger picture. And then, at some point, the piece appears that changes everything.

The moment that sparks this epiphany, as with so many other insights on our unschooling journey, may be quite ordinary. But this one, for some reason, is the puzzle piece that gives you that flash of insight. All of a sudden you can see the picture you're building and how the various pieces fit together. Where earlier on your journey you probably thought that no longer judging situations would muddy the waters intolerably (does that mean everything is "good?"), almost paradoxically, you see things more clearly now. The naivete of our urge to judge becomes apparent and our understanding of the value of all experiences—good, bad, and otherwise—rises out the confusing free-for-all we first envisioned.

How does this play out in our days? It doesn't mean that no more bad moments happen in our lives—our lives go on as they ever did—but our perspective has changed. Fear loses much of its power. We stop desperately trying to avoid or escape bad moments, understanding that they, while not what we hoped for, are just moments. We grow to trust ourselves to handle whatever kind of moment comes our way. A beautiful sense of confidence begins to take root as we more mindfully engage in all the moments of our days. And we see our children living this trust and confidence—it's something humans are born knowing, but we lost track of growing up immersed in judgement, shame, and fear. As always, the children are our guides.

And then it hits us: life isn't about trying to avoid "bad" moments so we can finally live our "good" lives. We've been living our full lives all along.

EMBRACING THE VALUE OF TIME

On this more spiritual leg of the journey, we're digging deeper. When we start a new stage, often we understand the concept intellectually, but I encourage you not to stop there. There's a deeper level of understanding that you'll reach as you continue to poke and prod, looking at the ideas from this way and that. Up close and far away. That's why deschooling takes time. The typical guideline is a month for each year of schooling, and, as adults, we've probably had at least twelve years of school, so, expect to be actively deschooling for at least a year, though I suspect you'll never be done. I'm not.

If you are persistent, you will reach deeper levels of understanding, moving from comprehension (the ideas make sense), to experience (you've seen the ideas in action with your children), and then to truth (you've seen them play out multiple times, in multiple circumstances). I encourage you to revisit many of these unschooling ideas again in six months, a year, two years from now, and I bet you'll be delighted to find that you understand them more deeply.

This stage is a great example of this. If discovering the truths around learning and parenting in the last two stages was akin to adding new landmarks to your map, this stage was about taking the time to explore them more fully, eventually revealing the secluded trails that connect them. We also get our first taste of the fruits of this inner journey: releasing the need to be constantly judging things is so freeing!

Time is a priceless and integral component of both our journey to understand and embrace unschooling and of the practice of unschooling itself. Seeing the value of time in our lives, and in our children's lives, and relinquishing our need to control and manipulate it, has enabled us to put together the puzzle pieces that make up this bigger picture truth about life. The insight I gained on this leg of the journey was incredibly valuable.

We've gone from intellectually understanding that life encompasses good and bad moments, to experiencing the learning about the world and about ourselves that is found in both kinds of moments, to embracing the truth that all moments—good, bad and all manner of in between moments—have value. We've also seen how all these moments are connected in the bigger picture of time, informing each other as they flow through the ups and downs of our days. When we are choosing our experiences, no matter their outcome, what we learn from them shapes us into the person we want to be moving forward. We are always learning. Through the ups and the downs. Through the good and the bad. It's life.

Or, as Campbell describes it, the nature of being.

~ STAGE NINE ~

ACCEPTING OUR NATURE

TEMPTATION IS NOT FAILURE.

Welcome to the next stage. How are you doing?

You've come a long way on your journey—maybe you've been unschooling for months, probably longer. I imagine you're feeling a level of competence in the world of unschooling, and that's great! So, what's ahead for us now on our path?

This stage is all about the temptations from our old lives that may lead us to abandon or stray from our unschooling quest. Our lives have probably changed quite a bit since we were living in our ordinary world, but, chances are, reality rarely matches what we first envisioned our unschooling lives would look like. In his book, *Essential Zen Habits*, Leo Babauta, an unschooling dad who writes a lot about changing habits on his blog zenhabits.net, calls this the Mind Movie: the stories and images we play over and over again in our heads and become attached to. These are our fantasies and expectations detailing what we think our unschooling lives should be. (One thing I've learned is that whenever I hear the word "should" in my head, it's a pretty reliable clue that I'm thinking in terms of fantasy rather than reality.)

THE NATURE OF TEMPTATION

Looking back, there were many days when life was exciting and wonderful. But they weren't all that way. There were days when my mind was replaying the almost utopian unschooling life I fantasized about when I first began learning about unschooling while our actual days were stubbornly following a different script. And when I was stuck in my mind movie and things got challenging, sometimes I'd experience the pull of temptation to step off the path. We were far enough away from our old lives that I'd feel a twinge of almost nostalgia for the seeming relative ease of doing things the same way as everyone else—with parents in control and children learning according to the conventional timetable.

Maybe the challenge was sibling arguments.

Why can't they get along? Wouldn't it be easier to just send them to their rooms?

Maybe it was a child immersed in a previously controlled or limited activity.

Why won't he do other things? That can't be good for him. Would it be better if we insist he does something else for a while?

Or maybe it was a child's learning.

Is she really learning anything useful? Maybe our child is different; maybe she won't learn the important things without being taught?

At first, we want to ignore our growing frustration with the situation. We keep ourselves busy with other things, and maybe we find ourselves biting our tongue more and more often. Still, ignoring things doesn't work for long—the challenges seem to follow us around, confronting us at every turn.

This isn't the way things are supposed to go. Surely things should be getting easier by now. Why do things seem to be going off the rails? We worked so hard to get here!

Once we can no longer ignore the issue, we feel exposed, sure everyone else can see it too. Then the fear of being judged a failure has us quickly looking around for someone else to blame, passing responsibility around like a hot potato. It's not our fault, we rationalize.

Maybe we're tempted to blame the experienced unschoolers we know (in person or online) who made their lives seem so wonderful—obviously, they aren't sharing what goes on behind closed doors. Or maybe the temptation is to blame our children's friends for bringing enticing things like video games into our lives—the neighbours are the bad guys. Maybe we're even tempted to blame our children, explaining to ourselves that our kids are more difficult than most—experienced unschoolers must have kids who are easier to manage, who easily go along with whatever comes up. In time, our frustrations grow into fears and soon we may be sorely tempted to declare the journey a bust, quit unschooling, and retreat to our ordinary world.

But do these frustrations and fears really mean we aren't cut out for unschooling? Maybe. Maybe not. Certainly, doing battle with our inner demons is hard. In fact, when we find ourselves here, it might help to remind ourselves that inner change like this is so universally hard that the temptation to turn back has its own stage in the hero's journey! We are not alone.

THE TEMPTATIONS OF THE BUDDHA

As is common with mythological tales, there are many different versions of the story surrounding Buddha's encounter with the demon Mara, but, details aside, it speaks well to temptations that try to lure us off our path.

~ ~ ~

Siddhartha Gautama was born in the 5th century BCE, in what is now Nepal, and grew up a sheltered prince. At the age of 29, he decided to leave the family palace and, for the first time, encountered human suffering. He met an old man, a sick man, a dead man, and an ascetic (a monk who renounces material and physical pleasures). These events eventually became known as the Four Sights. Soon after, Prince Siddhartha, deeply troubled by the suffering he saw, and curious about the monk's happy and peaceful demeanour, left home and undertook a spiritual journey as a wandering ascetic.

He studied with renown yoga teachers, learning all he could from one before moving on to the next. He also spent time practicing rigorous asceticism through strict physical discipline, including near starvation. Yet, he felt enlightenment still eluded him. Then, recalling a time when, as a young boy, he had experienced a deep peace in meditation, he realized that there was a Middle Way, a path between the extreme self-indulgence of his youth and the extreme self-denial of asceticism. It was through the discipline of the mind.

After regaining some strength, Siddhartha Gautama sat cross-legged beneath a sacred fig tree and began to meditate. As he strove for enlightenment, purifying his mind through concentration, a demon, Mara the Tempter, appeared, determined to thwart his efforts. It is said that first Mara brought his three beautiful daughters to tempt Siddhartha away from his work through the pleasures of the flesh, but he was not swayed. Next Mara brought forth armies of demons, trying to provoke Siddhartha's anger and break his concentration, but as they attacked, the power of his concentration turned their hurtling weapons into flowers, which fell harmlessly to the ground. Finally, Mara challenged Siddhartha's claim to the seat of enlightenment and demanded proof that he was worthy. In response, Siddhartha touched the earth with his right hand and the earth itself spoke on his behalf, bearing witness to his claim. And with that, Mara and his army disappeared.

Having weathered Mara's temptations, Siddhartha sunk even deeper into his meditation. In time, the meaning of all things became clear and he realized enlightenment, becoming Buddha, the Awakened One. Feeling great compassion for humanity, he shared his understanding of the Four Noble Truths and the Eightfold Path to end suffering and gain enlightenment. This practice became known as Buddhism.

~ ~ ~

ACCEPTING OURSELVES IS OUR AWAKENING

One of the important insights in this stage is the realization that even though we may try to blame others for our discomfort, our frustrations are really about us, not them. The particular set of challenges that we meet in this stage to tempt us to abandon our journey will be unique to each of us—they are the demons that we personally need to conquer on our own inner journey. Meaning, they'll keep confronting us until we can no longer ignore them.

So, as Mara attempted to distract Siddhartha away from his path with companionship, we too may be tempted to distract ourselves by keeping busy so we can avoid sitting alone with our frustrations, temptations, and feelings. We might also find ourselves tempted to view our challenges in terms of conflict—a perspective Mara tried to elicit in Siddhartha. When we see things through the lens of conflict, judgement and blame become the tools of choice, and our fears push us to protect ourselves by blaming others. And, as when Mara demanded proof of Siddhartha's claim in hopes that he would abandon his journey, we too may fall prey to the voices in our heads demanding we prove unschooling is working. Maybe we're tempted to exert just a bit of control, cajoling our children into doing a couple of worksheets—just to "prove" they are learning. If we fall prey to these temptations, we are stepping off our unschooling path.

Granted, it's not the end of the world if that happens. It's much like landing on a snake in a game of Snakes and Ladders—you slide back on your journey and have some more work to do. Temptation wins for a while, but it needn't mark the permanent end of your journey. It's worth the effort to figure out what happened and get back on the path. It's living and learning and growing. I mentioned this is hard, right?

So, where can we find help in this stage? All together now: our guides! Most definitely. So often we can see patterns more clearly in our children than we can in ourselves. Those conventional voices in our head continue to hound us if we give them the slightest opening—and feeling tempted to give up on our journey is just such an opening. But, in my experience, they aren't so loud when it comes to my children. When I paid attention, I saw them wrestling with challenges, fears, and temptations to quit on their learning paths and it didn't take me long to realize that those moments were all valuable aspects of their journey, not things gone wrong. And eventually, I was able to extend that kindness to myself.

These are the fallen logs on our path that lead us to discover the beautiful river running thirty feet away through the forest, where we can quench our thirst and rest for a time, quietly within ourselves. I came to understand that the feeling of temptation to stray from a quest—any quest—was not a failure in me. I realized that the point wasn't for me to "get strong enough" so that I would never be tempted again, but to understand that these moments are part of life, of being human. And from there I could more quickly and compassionately recognize them for what they were—messages about me, and for me—so I could do the work to move through them.

I came to accept all facets of myself—the confident me, the fearful me, the tempted me—and no longer judged them as "good" and "bad," but saw and accepted them all as part of my nature.

LIVING MINDFULLY

With time and experience, I learned to recognize these moments of temptation more quickly and I found my most useful tool was the idea of living mindfully. To me, that means being curious and paying attention to what's going on around me, letting go of expectations and the need to control things, becoming okay with discomfort, noticing my own feelings of resistance to some things and urges to do other things, and appreciating the many things around me that I'm grateful for, big and small.

When I stopped judging myself for having these moments of fear or temptation, I also stopped trying to distance myself from them by blaming others, and eventually, I was able to sit with my discomfort for a while. Discomfort became, maybe not my good friend, but definitely not my enemy.

In her book, *The Wisdom of No Escape* (2001), Pema Chödrön, an American Buddhist nun wrote: "Our neurosis and our wisdom are made out of the same material. If you throw out your neurosis, you also throw out your wisdom" (Popova, 2015). But, if you don't throw out your neurosis—your frustration, fear, and discomfort—what do you do with them? How do you discover the wisdom that is tangled up in there? Maria Popova (2015), founder of BrainPickings.org, expanded eloquently on Chödrön's intent: "Holding one's imperfection with gentleness is not the same as resignation or condoning harmful behaviour—rather, it's a matter of befriending imperfection rather than banishing it, in order to then gently let it go rather than forcefully expel it."

As I sat kindly with my unease, I learned what I could about myself and the roots of my needs and desires—what was behind my fantasy mind movie—and then gently let go of the leftover bits I no longer wanted. The pieces that didn't mesh with the person and parent I wanted to be.

SITTING WITH DISCOMFORT TO DISCOVER
WHAT TO LET GO

I remember back when my three children were ages ten and under and, with them now home all day, their boundless energy was in turns amazingly beautiful and overwhelming. Keeping up with them was both inspiring and exhausting, leaving practically no time for anything else, including things that I wanted to do. I would also hear messages to moms, especially of younger kids, to take time for themselves. It seemed to apply precisely to my situation, yet it didn't feel good to me either. I was stuck in that feeling of overwhelm and growing frustration, not seeing any way through it to the other side.

So, I sat with my discomfort. As I dug into it, I found that I felt like I could never get a break; that it was all kids, all the time. I felt like I was a mom all the time and didn't have time to be me. When I found that thought, it seemed like I was finally getting somewhere, that I'd caught a glimpse of the root of my discomfort. I kept digging. Why are "mom" and "me" two different things? Am I a different person when I'm with my kids? Is "mother" a role I'm playing? I'm thinking of my life as divided into two slices: time with the kids when I meet their needs and ignore mine; and time without the kids when I meet my needs and can ignore theirs. And I keep looking for time without the kids so I can finally meet my needs, without actually leaving the kids. No wonder that wasn't working!

Once I found the root of the issue—the two thoughts that were at odds with each other—I could figure out which one was really true for me. What kind of parent do I want to be? I don't want to be a parent that feels she needs to escape her kids to be her true self—I want to be myself even when I'm with my kids. I don't want to view "mother" as a role I play; it is an integral part of me. And my needs, the things that nurture me, are also an integral part of me. That meant that the thought that wasn't working for me, the one to gently let go of, was that I needed time without the kids to meet my needs.

Sweet! I understood where it came from—it was a piece of parenting wisdom that I'd come across regularly—but now I knew that it was yet another piece of conventional advice that I wanted to release, and why. When I understand my why, not only can I brainstorm ways to address the root of the issue, I can more quickly walk myself through it if—and more probably, when—this issue resurfaces. Remember, this isn't a battle to judge, overpower, and eliminate parts of ourselves; it's about accepting that these ups and downs are part of our nature. And learning that with understanding, self-awareness, and knowing the tools that work for us, we can move through these down moments with much more grace.

And then, without the constraint of the belief that I need to find alone time to fully be myself—needs included—the possibilities opened up! I realized that this separation between being me and being a mother was actually being fed by the conventional presumption that being a full-time parent was second-class work.

You'll be bored spending all day with your kids if you don't turn off half your brain and look forward to time away from your kids to replenish the real you.

See how they feed each other? I thought I valued my work as a mother before this stage, but now I understood it at a whole new level. Once I decided to bring my full self to each day without judgement, I found so many real reasons why I would choose to get on the floor and play face to face with my children. To take them to the park. To make messes with them.

I also started looking for ways to share and nurture other aspects of myself, while being with my children. For me, sometimes it was suggesting puzzle games—my favourite kind of game. Or reading a magazine nearby as they played or watched TV. Or reaching for an almost meditative state during repetitive activities like pushing a swing, or separating Lego pieces. A candle lit in the kitchen while I tidied or prepared food. A light nap as they were engrossed in a movie. A walk around the block giving us all new things to look at, including me appreciating the neighbours' front gardens and maybe picking up some ideas. A quiet coffee and a book for a half hour before the kids woke up. The whole me is always there and these activities were re-energizing.

I was no longer desperately looking for alone time to replenish myself. I brought all of me to my days with my kids, and when I wanted time alone or with friends, I arranged that—not as an escape from them, but as part of being me. When I was the mom and the person I wanted to be at the same time, my days became more expansive and I felt more fully myself for the first time in a long time.

UNDERCURRENT OF JOY

In this stage, we learn to accept, rather than fight, our nature. We move beyond judging ourselves so that we can mindfully move through these moments of temptation, learn what we can, and continue on our journey. And it doesn't stop there! In this deeper acceptance of myself and the resulting freer flow of our days, I discovered an undercurrent of joy running through our lives. Like a subterranean river flowing beneath all of our experiences and through all my different states of mind. This is yet another aspect of the flow of time we discussed in the last stage. Another aspect of the nature of being.

This more expansive lens of time inspired another shift in my perspective on lifelong learning. Learning is not the work of childhood. Learning truly can happen at any age—this was a deeper level of understanding I found in the unschooling truth that children are always learning. It grew to humans are always learning.

As my fears faded, I realized that, in the grand scheme of things, most unpleasant/distressing moments aren't as dire as they first appear. I found I could be more present with both happiness and disappointment in those moments, as Maria described, without taking an internal roller coaster ride because I no longer equated the deep, longer-term sense of joy I felt inside with the emotions of the moments I was in. And I discovered that my joy was rooted in knowing more deeply that I was in control of my life—no one else. I was free to make the choices that made sense to me without judging myself. And there I was, back, full circle.

Looking back now, I realize that I instinctively understood the immense value and beauty of our days once I discovered that undercurrent of joy, long before I discovered the concept of the hero's journey. I know that because, way back in 2004, two years after the start of my unschooling journey, I incorporated it into my website name: livingjoyfully.ca.

~ STAGE TEN ~

ACCEPTING OTHERS WHERE THEY ARE

SEEING OURSELVES IN OTHERS.

Stop for a moment and take a deep breath. Maybe two. Are you ready to forge ahead?

All the work we've done on our journey so far has prepared us for this stage. We will need all our wits about us as we probe the remaining power imbalance in our lives. We have big questions to ask ourselves. Who still holds power over us? How? Why? Where does it come from? Why do we continue to engage with them on the see-saw of resisting their power and seeking their approval?

Do you see how those two ideas live on the same continuum? We resist their control in our lives; we want to make our own choices. On the other hand, we desperately want their approval. Even though we suspect it's futile, we catch ourselves needing to convince them we are right, that our unschooling choice is a good one. If we could just find the right thing to say that will persuade them. But deep down we know that the only path to their approval is to do what they want us to do. And each time we remember this it spurs us to again resist their power over us. The see-saw goes up and down, up and down. This is the ride we've lived on, probably since the start of our journey, but now we're ready to find the exit. Though it may not be the way we expect.

Campbell calls this stage "Atonement with the Father." This authority figure represents whatever the hero—that's you—sees as the ultimate power in their life. Who, or what, has the power to make you feel small? As you contemplate that, think back to stage four, when we were crossing the threshold to the world of unschooling. I asked you to remember whose voice you heard in your head as you read through the typical conversation with a threshold guardian. That voice may be a clue to who continues to hold sway over you.

THE NEED TO BE RIGHT

To explore this stage, we're going to look at both ends of this power-based see-saw. On one end are the times when we are feeling reasonably self-assured as we engage with others; we can resist their attempts to exert power over us. We feel confident that our choices are good ones. And at some point, after trying to help a friend with a challenge, I imagine most of us have thought, or maybe even said, "If only they'd listen to me, their life would be so much easier!" Maybe followed by a sigh or a slight shake of the head. It's not usually said with any particular malice. We are earnestly sharing our advice, hoping they'll take it. We are confident it will work for them because, if we found ourselves in that situation, those are the actions we'd take and they'd most likely work out well for us.

But something interesting happened when I found myself in that moment and chose to dig deeper. I asked myself why the person was so resistant. Why didn't my suggestions make sense to them? They certainly made sense to me. And then it eventually hit me: yes, I was seeing the situation clearly, but through my personal filters. I was assuming that those choices would be best for the other person too.

But human beings aren't interchangeable clones. We cannot feel the signals from someone else's body—their relaxed or racing heart, the hair rising on the back of their neck in awe or fear, or the adrenalin pumping with excitement. We can't know the memories being triggered—from last week or from a decade ago. We can't know the goals that lie deep in their heart, yet to be shared with anyone.

And, again, I discovered these bigger picture insights about life through watching my children's unschooling lives unfold. I saw them making choices that, looking through their eyes, were clearly wonderfully perfect choices for them! But when I put myself in their shoes, I would never have made the same choices. It's such a subtle but essential shift in perspective.

I came to see the profound difference between putting myself in another person's shoes and thinking about what I would do, and seeing a situation through their eyes and contemplating what they might want to do. There are probably as many different workable paths forward as there are people involved in a given situation! As I began letting go of thinking I knew better than others about their own lives, the need to convince them to do things my way, "for their own good," faded. Pretty soon the idea of judging someone else's choices as right or wrong, or telling them in no uncertain terms what they should do in a situation, felt very uncomfortable.

This often also translates to another level of release and trust with our children. Remember those deeper levels of understanding we reach with time and experience? But here's where we can sometimes flounder. When we no longer feel the need to get in the middle of things and exert some control over the situation, we sometimes step too far away from their lives and risk becoming disconnected. Yes, it's not about unduly influencing—controlling—our children's choices, but it's also not about leaving them to figure things out on their own. We are an integral part of their journey.

Life is the dance of everything in between. I was still involved in their days. I chose my next steps—backward, forward, to the side—in response to their steps, and to the nuance of the moment. Was the music picking up or slowing down? Was it time to follow or lead? I could commiserate with those involved, sometimes sharing my thoughts and the subtleties of the situation as I saw them, as well as brainstorm possibilities and any pros and cons I envisioned from their perspective. And, if asked, I could even share what I'd probably do in similar circumstances.

I no longer felt the need to attach any expectations to the outcome. Nor would I feel slighted if they chose a different path forward because I knew, in that case, there were probably pieces of the puzzle I was missing. Maybe even that everyone was missing. We do our best in the moment and see what happens. And because this way of engaging with my children felt so right and made so much sense, soon I was treating the adults in my life the same way: I didn't know better than they did what they needed. If asked, I could share what I saw, even brainstorm ideas with them, but I could leave it there.

Their choices weren't about me at all.

THE NEED FOR APPROVAL

So, where does this release of attachment to others' choices and outcomes lead us? Well, now we have a new perspective on things as we dig even deeper and come face to face with our authority figure. We soon realize that the one whose approval we have been seeking is also seeing situations through their filters. Interesting!

Now we better understand why they are so sure their way is the right way. Chances are, they are putting themselves in our shoes, rather than looking at the situation from our perspective—through our eyes and our circumstances. With that understanding, we come to realize that their suggestions say more about where they are on their journey than they do about where we are on ours. As that revelation solidifies, the impact of their judgmental pronouncements fades—it's not really about us at all. Soon, their comments sail right past us rather than hitting us in the solar plexus. Power struggles dissolve because we no longer feel defensive. Nor do we feel the need to rush them along on their journey. Instead, we can meet them where they are. We realize their path may be different than ours. The need for their approval slowly evaporates. They will get there in their own time. Or not.

At the same time, we are very comfortable with our choices, and now that seems to be enough.

We finally step off the see-saw.

ACCEPTING OTHERS WHERE THEY ARE

My authority figure, the one whose power to judge and shame me held out the longest, was not an individual but society. My parents, while they didn't particularly understand unschooling, weren't against it. Sometimes they asked questions, and we would chat, but it wasn't confrontational. I felt their trust. What did manage to make me feel unworthy and defensive for the longest time were the pointed glances of passing acquaintances, usually in group situations. People who knew my kids didn't go to school but knew little about us. It was clear they thought I was foolish. Before going into those group situations, I would give myself a bit of a pep talk, reminding myself that they knew little about our lives and that unschooling was working well for us. Even after countless internal pep talks, I still felt uneasy. And the memory of when that changed is still fresh, so many years later. It was a clear turning point for me—though I didn't realize it was *this* particular turning point until I dived into Campbell's work.

We were in a school gym and I and a dozen or so other moms were huddled around the Girl Guide troop leader. It was a few days before Lissy's first overnight camp, and the leader was explaining the camp rules. She also had a couple of questions for us: "Do you give me permission to let your daughter call you from camp? And can she ask to be picked up?"

All the other moms said, "No, my daughter has to stay for the whole camp," and "No, she can't call home." The relief was palpable in some of their voices. They were plainly grateful for the opportunity to pass on to someone else the responsibility of saying no to their daughters, pre-emptively avoiding any guilt-inducing phone calls home. We all knew that bringing a child home early would be seen by the other moms as a parenting failure. A bit unexpectedly, I felt a connection with them because I well knew that pulse-quickening moment when the possibility of impending judgement pops up and the anxious wish to avoid the resulting shame.

When it was my turn, I just said, "Sure, she can call me. And yes, I'll come get her if she wants." In my mind, I knew I didn't want her to feel left alone to fend for herself if she decided she wanted my help. I recall that, despite feeling a connection with some of the other moms, I was a bit surprised that nobody else said yes. But this time I didn't feel like their answers were wrong. I do remember feeling very comfortable with my answer, and the fact that it would probably be perceived as a failure on my part by the other moms didn't faze me at all. I distinctly remember the dawning realization that I felt no need to apologize for my choice, nor to explain it. It was just the best choice for us, and I was happy to take full responsibility for it. It felt refreshing. Relaxing. Peaceful even. I saw everyone making the choice they wanted. And I didn't need to know how the weekend played out for other families because it didn't matter—those were their lives to learn from, not mine to meddle or judge. How could I know the nuances at play in their lives?

As for us, Lissy called. And I picked her up. At midnight. It turned out to be a wonderful, bonding moment. She was grateful when I arrived, and, with another example that I would happily be there to support her choices, her trust in me grew. We had a lovely conversation on the way home. She slept in her bed, feeling safe and cared for. As I imagine, so did the girls that were excited to stay at camp.

Next time there was a camp, Lissy chose to go. I answered the questions the same way. She didn't call. I would have gone if she did.

We are all on the same journey, creating our unique paths as we make the choices that feel best for us in the moment. Our choices play out however they do, and we can learn from them. Or not. In that moment, I deeply felt what Campbell calls the "at-one-ment" of this atonement stage. I no longer felt they had any power over me, and my internal struggles faded. In fact, I felt empowered to go against the rules and norms of conventional society and take full responsibility for doing so. I no longer felt I had to hide my actions to protect myself. I felt more fully myself than I had in a long time.

SIMBA CHOOSES TO TAKE HIS PLACE IN THE CIRCLE OF LIFE

In the story of *The Lion King* (Allers and Minkoff), a Disney movie released in 1994, there is a beautiful scene depicting this stage of atonement with the father. Here's a quick summary of the story leading up to that scene to get us situated. I'm sure by now you'll recognize some of the earlier stages of Simba's journey.

As a cub, Simba was tricked by his uncle, Scar, into thinking he was responsible for the death of his beloved father, Mufasa, King of the Pride Lands. Immediately after, Scar convinces Simba to run away (and sends his hyenas to follow and kill him) and takes over as the new King. Escaping the hyenas, Simba arrives in his new world and finds allies in Timon and Pumba, who teach him all about their *hakuna matata* lifestyle. Time passes, and, now an adult, Simba runs into his childhood best friend, Nala. She explains that Scar has let the hyenas take over the Pride Lands and they are now desolate. She urges him to return home and take his rightful place as King. Simba, still believing he caused his father's death, feels too ashamed to consider returning home, to his social community—his pride (a great name for a group of lions!).

And now we have the scene where everything changes for Simba. He meets Rafiki, a mentor figure, who tells Simba that his father is still alive—in him. How much more "at one with your father" can you get than seeing your father's face in yours as you gaze at your reflection in the water? Mufasa's ghost then appears in the sky, and he speaks with Simba, imploring him to remember who he is and to take his place in the Circle of Life.

Simba is clearly deeply moved by the encounter, seeing that his father wants him to assume his role even after all that's happened and feeling that kinship, that oneness, with his father. When Rafiki reappears, Simba remarks that the winds are changing.

Rafiki says, "Change is good."

And Simba replies, "Yeah, but it's not easy. I know what I have to do. But, going back means I'll have to face my past. I've been running from it for so long."

Change is not easy. But Simba is now ready to rejoin his community. He understands that they may judge him negatively, but now he can accept that—and them. He no longer fears them because now he understands who he is, and he's ready to be himself. Everywhere.

SHOWING UP OPENLY

It was a powerful scene, and watching it now, the similarities with my own moment of revelation are striking. For years, Simba resisted returning to his community because he was ashamed of his role in his father's death. I resisted openly engaging with my community because I felt the roller coaster of shame in their obvious disdain for my family's choice not to send our kids to school. But both Simba and I met a moment when that resistance faded. We understood now that they were people on their own journeys, making their own choices, just as we were. And we were no longer ashamed to show up openly as ourselves, mistakes and all, doing our best.

Over the last three stages we've undergone some profound transformations, and together they've formed a sequence of ever-deepening acceptance. First, we moved beyond the desire to judge situations as good or bad, right or wrong, and accepted the value of all experiences. Next, we moved beyond judging ourselves, accepting our nature, so we can more gracefully move through the inevitable moments of temptation we will continue to encounter. And, in this last stage, we moved beyond resistance and shame stemming from other people's judgement of us—and conversely, the need to judge them—to become comfortable accepting them where they are on their own journey. As our need for the approval of the remaining authority figure fades, so does the last of our power struggles.

As we continue to embrace this new level of self-awareness, we no longer feel the need to hide or apologize for our choices, nor are we drawn to flaunt them—we just live them. In the end, we realize that we hold the ultimate power in our life.

And only in our life.

~ STAGE ELEVEN ~

CULTIVATING KINDNESS AND COMPASSION

FINDING THE MAGIC IN THE MESS.

Joseph Campbell calls this stage "Apotheosis": rising to the rank of a god. In other words, reaching our highest level. For example, we might say a particular movie was the apotheosis of an actor's career. On the hero's journey, this stage describes when the hero moves beyond the last pockets of ignorance and reaches a divine state.

As we contemplate what we've learned about judgement, temptation, and power over the last three stages of our journey, our understanding continues to grow, and in this stage, we glimpse the true nature of life. We discover the wholeness that generously encompasses both poles of opposites: yes and no, right and wrong, good and bad, birth and death, time and eternity, us and them, yin and yang.

YIN AND YANG

In Chinese philosophy, yin and yang describe how seemingly opposite forces are actually interconnected and complementary. Yin represents the dark, passive, feminine side while yang is the light, active, masculine side. In Chinese mythology, yin and yang were born out of chaos, such as in the creation story of P'an Ku (or Pangu). One version begins with a cosmic egg floating in the void containing the chaos energy of the universe. (In fact, many cultures have creation myths that begin with some version of a cosmic egg.)

~ ~ ~

P'an Ku evolved inside an enormous cosmic egg, growing ten feet each day. As he grew, he gradually separated the forces of nature into their opposites: earth (yin) and sky (yang); light (yang) and dark (yin); wet (yin) and dry (yang); male (yang) and female (yin) and so on. After 18,000 years he was fully grown, and the separation was complete. The egg hatched, and P'an Ku died. His eyes became the sun and the moon, his body became the features of the earth, his sweat became the water, and the tiny fleas on his body became people.

~ ~ ~

The modern yin/yang symbol represents how these complementary opposites—yin/black and yang/white—energetically swirl together. One waxes while the other wanes, each, in turn, reaching their fullest expression while the seed of its opposite dwells deep in its core. They are mutually dependent on each other—forever shifting, but together, an indivisible whole. Neither is superior. The dynamic tension and flow between them expresses the cosmic harmony of the universe. Two aspects of one reality.

This reminds us that there is a duality in all things and that there is value at every point in between polar opposites. That fits so well with much of what we've discovered on our journey, doesn't it? The spectrum of possibilities that lie between yes and no. The learning about the world and ourselves that happens whether things turn out good or bad. Neither result is superior; it is all valuable experience. When we—we and our children—are choosing our actions and learning from our experiences, we grow into the people that we want to be. There is value and learning in all states, and the yin/yang symbol expresses this beautifully.

UNITY AND DUALITY IN STORY

Remember, story is to humans as water is to fish. It is instinctual. A well-told story needs a sense of oneness, of unity, which is expressed through its theme, its one overarching idea. Yet, a good story also needs an aspect of duality: the push and pull of opposites that add tension and movement.

Christopher Vogler explains this well in his book, *The Writer's Journey* (2007): "As soon as you choose a single thought or character to unite your story, you have automatically generated its polar opposite, a contrary concept or antagonistic character, and therefore a duality or polarized system that conducts energy between the two parties. Unity begets duality; the existence of one implies the possibility of two."

P'an Ku split the cosmic energy to create a world of opposites, yet we need one to define the other. You can't have wet without dry. Light without dark. Up without down. Trust without suspicion. Forgiveness without revenge. And in story, as in life, change is constant. That waxing and waning flow of energy between the poles makes for great stories because it connects to us on a deep level. It is an expression of human nature. Even if we can't name it, we can feel it. A satisfying story connects with us on an instinctual level.

APPROACHING THE SUMMIT

What about our unschooling story? We've explored opposites extensively and come to understand the overarching unity that encompasses them both. How do we bring this sense of oneness into our days? As we begin to actively embrace this wholeness rather than its parts, we experience the reality of living and learning in connection with our children more deeply and truly than we have before. As we continue to heal from our past, old fears and hurts fall away, and their influence on our choices fades. As that weight lifts, we feel lighter and more open, able to find more creative and fun ways to navigate our days. As our self-awareness grows, we bring more of our true selves into our days. And as we learn more about our children, our connection with them deepens, and our trust grows.

These revelations feed off each other, bringing an increasing lightness and depth to our days and in time we realize we are approaching the summit of our journey. Our apotheosis. When we look at others—in and out of our family—we see that they are on their own journeys, just as we are. From this vantage point, we see others as an integral part of the wholeness of our lives, and that we are an integral part of theirs. We see the whole of the yin/yang symbol, without favouring black or white. Our sense of "otherness," of "us versus them," fades. We are all human beings. We feel a growing sense of oneness, a kinship, with humanity.

KINDNESS AND COMPASSION

A few stages ago we talked about shifting our relationships with our children from control to connection, and we began not only putting ourselves in our children's shoes, but also seeing the world through their eyes—and not just their outer world, but their inner world too—and meeting them where they are. That ability to empathize with others, along with our growing sense of kinship with humanity, creates a rich soil in which kindness and compassion now begin to flourish. When we see ourselves in others, we can more easily choose to treat them, and ourselves, with kindness and compassion.

When Lissy was in her early teens, she came across a quote that struck her deeply: "Be kind, for everyone you meet is fighting a hard battle." One day we were chatting about decorating the basement, and she wanted to put that quote up somewhere. I picked up some large sticky-note letters, and we put the saying up on a wall, placing the words around a window frame. It's still there. Over the years it's been a touchstone for me, a reminder when I pass it to take the time to see things from the other person's perspective.

This was an insight that my children regularly brought me back to. There were times when I felt my children were wronged in some big or small way by another child, yet when we started chatting about it, the conversation would sometimes go in a very different direction than I anticipated. They knew the other child better than I did and would explain their actions with an understanding of the other child's circumstances and personality that would sometimes take my breath away. More instances where giving space to our conversations and letting my children direct the flow led to more learning and growing for me.

The small daily battles, the larger life-changing battles, all the questions and choices that appear on our plates each day—everyone has them. And no matter their family circumstances, their parenting styles, or what you think about their challenges, they are big and meaningful to them. They are the tricksters, monsters, and obstacles that are part of their life's journey and they are making choices that make the most sense to them. What they learn from these encounters is not under our control.

Those moms I mentioned in the last stage who chose to insist their daughters stay at camp? When we ran into each other at meetings in the future, I smiled at them with kindness. I nodded my head compassionately in conversation as they shared their frustrations with school or with their children. Acknowledging their truth in that moment does not say I would take the same actions. It says I hear you.

And in my experience, when people feel heard—when they are heard and acknowledged with kindness and compassion—sometimes there's this wonderful shift in their body language from tension to openness and the conversation takes a step deeper. Maybe they ask, "What would you do?" and I can share a perspective that is more child centred. With no expectation that it will be a sweeping revelation for them, or that they change their path. It's just a seed planted.

A Policy of Kindness (1990) is an anthology of writings by and about the Dalai Lama, and in a talk titled "Kindness and Compassion," he shared: "This is my simple religion. There is no need for temples; no need for complicated philosophy. Our own brain, our own heart is our temple; the philosophy is kindness."

He explained that while we've made startling advances in science and technology that have led to incredible levels of external progress, our internal progress has not kept up. As human beings, we all want happiness and peace of mind, but we cannot achieve that through anger. The blueprint lies in our mind—where we choose our actions. And it is through choosing kindness, love, and compassion that an individual can achieve peace of mind. This peace of mind infuses their personal relationships, resulting in a peaceful family. More and more peaceful families can eventually bring this perspective to the national level, and then ultimately the international level, the stage on which the Dalai Lama speaks.

But for us, on our unschooling journey, we are taking that inner journey of the mind and spirit, exploring and discovering how human beings are wired to learn and grow and interact with one another, regardless of age. We are creating our blueprint. And what we learn through unschooling with our children applies not only to ourselves but also to people at large. To humanity.

FINDING THE MAGIC IN THE MESS

Of course, none of this means our lives are easy or perfect. There are messy kitchens, diverging needs, sibling arguments, lack of sleep, and big disappointments. Not to mention finding time for a shower. It's life in all its glory. In my experience, so often when we choose to reach for kindness and compassion in the moment, we discover magic. The moment turns, and we find ourselves going places more interesting, more fun, and more meaningful than we could have predicted or even imagined.

At first, it took a leap of faith to do it—when things feel out of control, every fibre of our being wants to rein things back under our control. But after a few times of managing to reach for kindness, I saw the beauty and magic of releasing that desire for control. And eventually it became easier.

One story I recall fondly happened in the aftermath of a big January snow storm. Lissy was maybe thirteen or fourteen and we had tickets to see a concert in the city, about an hour away. That morning the snow was falling heavily, and I was sure they would cancel the show—people were being told to stay home if possible. I was looking forward to settling in and hanging around the fire. Lissy had been looking forward to the show and was understandably disappointed. I told her that I was pretty sure they'd reschedule the show, so she wouldn't miss it, it would just be postponed. She kept checking the website, and by early afternoon they announced that the show was going to go on.

Lissy wanted to go, and I wanted to stay home. I imagined all the hurdles in our way, and it seemed like way too much work. But I saw her suffering, and I chose to react with compassion. And though I couldn't yet muster a "Yes, let's go!" I did manage to take a small step to meet her with "Maybe." Though the snow had stopped falling, I explained the obstacles I saw and that I was willing to try the next step and see how it looked. If it looked okay, we'd try the next step. And the next. She agreed.

Step one: Clean off the car and shovel enough of the driveway to get out by our planned departure time. We did it! Even after the snow plow went by and created another curb of snow at the end of the driveway.

Step two: Is our local rural road plowed and safely drivable? That was a yes too.

Step three: Pack the car with extra hats and mitts and snacks in case we get stuck along the way. Done. By the time we pulled out of the driveway, it felt like we were on quite the adventure! I was rather surprised we'd actually made it this far, but there was no point that said stop, so we kept going.

Step four: I reminded Lissy as we slowly drove into the city that if the roads or the traffic got bad, we'd turn back. Even in her excitement, she was fine with that. Turned out though the roads were snow covered they had been plowed, so it wasn't deep, and traffic was light. Slowly, but surely, we made our way into the city.

Step five: We pulled into the venue parking lot. We were both so surprised to find ourselves there! It was almost surreal. So white and quiet outside. And inside, the concert turned out to be a very intimate show. The band thanked those who showed up and really connected with the audience as they played. It ended up being a pretty magical night.

Time and again I've discovered that when things get messy, making an effort to reach for kindness and compassion pays dividends far beyond my investment. I have so many similar stories.

As you reach the summit of this stage, I suspect you will discover that when things are feeling off, there's no longer that fear-inspired adrenalin rush pushing you to grab control or to quickly blame someone else. Instead, you'll use your discomfort as a clue that you're probably missing a piece of the puzzle. Maybe it's more information about the situation or a better understanding of your children's perspective on it (their goal, their motivation, their understanding, and so forth). It doesn't mean ignoring your discomfort, rather learning to get to the root of it. Our lives are a dance of people sharing their needs and wants and motivations and doing what we can to help each other meet them.

Though sparked by our unschooling journey, this fundamental shift in perspective becomes a part of us, applicable to our whole lives, not just the unschooling bits. In fact, it's around this point that you may realize that there are no separate unschooling bits. Unschooling is life in all its messy beautifulness. And more and more often, we find ourselves living in wholeness, with kindness and compassion.

~ STAGE TWELVE ~

UNSCHOOLING WITH CONFIDENCE AND GRACE

UNSCHOOLING IS A PRACTICE.

As we crest the mountaintop, we obtain the holy grail of our quest: we are truly and deeply unschooling. This is what we set out to accomplish when we first answered the call to adventure. What we probably didn't realize back then was how winding and intense our journey was going to turn out to be! But as we survey the view from the summit, we know it was worth every step.

Our relationships with our children are steeped in connection and trust. We dance with them, sometimes leading, sometimes following, and sometimes even stepping on each other's toes—but we regroup and soon find our rhythm again. We are confidently living and learning together as a family. We trust the process of unschooling, now understanding that it is as simple—and as challenging—as living life. We are following our curiosity, developing our self-awareness, and pursuing our short- and long-term goals. We are mindfully engaged in our days, with all their ups and down and twists and turns. But now they are framed by the good-humoured joy we find in the everyday moments.

We've come to appreciate the beauty of the simplest moments: cuddling with our children on the couch watching a favourite movie; walking in the park, our kids darting from flower to flower, handing us the perfect rock to hold so they can add it to their collection when we get home; watching our child enthusiastically turn on the water to show us how it flows over the complicated contraption of pots and plates they've built in the sink; laying in bed together, reading a story out loud to them as their eyes blink heavily. These moments bring us deep joy and contentment. We know the power they hold.

THE ELIXIR OF GRACE

Campbell calls this stage "The Ultimate Boon," and, in myths and stories, the reward at the end of the journey is often represented by an object: fire, magical trinkets, priceless treasure, and elixirs of health or immortality. But after the trials and tribulations of the journey, the real reward isn't material. We have journeyed to attain the grace of the gods and goddesses. Not to steal it from them, nor to trick them into giving it to us—it's not a fixed commodity. But to come to understand, and therefore share, their perspective and their spirit. Their grace.

The goal is not to become a god or a goddess-like being. On our journey, we've learned to accept our human nature, to live mindfully in the moment, and not get caught up chasing some embodiment of perfection. There is no "perfect" model of unschooling; day-to-day, it looks different for everyone. But the principles of unschooling—the spirit with which unschooling is lived—is fundamentally the same. And that is what we've explored and absorbed on our journey.

Campbell describes our reward as the elixir of Imperishable Being, but it's not about immortality. The real prize the hero has gained is the knowledge of their indestructibility in life. It's that understanding, deep in our bones, that enables us to move through whatever challenges life throws at us. Grace is the kindness and compassion that comes from knowing that we will endure. That there is a light at the end of the tunnel, even if we can't quite see it yet.

It's not a case of thinking that when distressing things happen, it's "for our own good" or that "we deserve them." We don't feel the need to place blame, which adds a distorting filter to many situations. Hence, we see distressing events more clearly—more gracefully—and treat everyone involved kinder and more compassionately as we move through them. Our journey starts out focused on our children and ends up being a boon for ourselves: one that fully includes our children in its embrace. It has also grown beyond unschooling into the realm of life.

THE STORY OF PSYCHE AND EROS

The Greek myth of Psyche and Eros connects beautifully with the deschooling phase of our journey. "Psyche" is the Greek word for breath or soul and, in this story, Psyche is the personification of the soul. As we wrap up this phase, we recognize that much of our work here has been inner work, engaging deeply with our soul and exploring what it means to be human.

~ ~ ~

Psyche was a mortal, born to a king and queen, the youngest and the most beautiful of their three daughters. She was so beautiful that admirers began worshipping her, rather than Aphrodite, the goddess of love and beauty. When Aphrodite caught wind of this, she was not pleased. She dispatched her son, Eros, god of love and desire, with orders to prick Psyche with one of his arrows and ensure she falls in love with a loathsome creature. But just as he sees her, Eros accidentally pricks himself and immediately falls in love with her. He decides to take her as his bride and whisks her away to a beautiful house in a lovely valley. Psyche finds herself in paradise with a god for a husband, and she can have anything she wishes but with one restriction: she may not look at him nor ask anything about him. Each night he comes to her through the window, makes love to her, and leaves before morning.

Psyche's two older sisters, having heard she has married a god and lives in paradise, are incredibly jealous and keep asking to visit. Eventually, Eros agrees, and Psyche invites them. Filled with envy, they concoct a plan to break up the couple. They tell Psyche that her husband is actually a loathsome creature who will kill her, and they advise her to hide a lamp and a knife in the bedroom, and when he's asleep, use the lamp to see his true form and the knife to kill him. Psyche is taken in by their story and follows their instructions.

Sound familiar? On our journey, the sisters represent those nagging voices—the ones in our heads replaying the conventional messages we've grown up with, as well as the ones in our lives trying to scare us into abandoning our journey.

~ ~ ~

That night, Psyche uncovers the lamp and sees her husband for the first time. She discovers he is the god of love! In her shock, she accidentally pricks herself with one of his arrows and falls in love with him. In the commotion, a drop of hot oil from the lamp falls on Eros and awakens him. When he sees what has happened, he takes flight out the window, Psyche grabbing hold of him. It's not long though before she loses her grip and falls to the ground. Eros lands nearby and tells her that she has broken her promise, and their paradise has been destroyed. He flies away.

Psyche is devastated and, consumed by love, sets out on a quest to find Eros. Eventually, she goes to Aphrodite's temple to pray for help. Aphrodite appears, and, still jealous, gives her four difficult tasks to complete.

For the first task, Aphrodite takes Psyche to a room with a huge pile of mixed grains and insists she have them all sorted by morning. Psyche is overwhelmed and sees no way that she can complete the task on time.

~ ~ ~

This task reminds me of when I first crossed the threshold into the world of unschooling, that feeling of being overwhelmed with all my questions, not knowing which to pursue first. But really, all we can do is get started. Pick one question, one grain—any one—and sort it out. Then the next one. And the next.

~ ~ ~

Soon, ants appear and begin to help Psyche sort the grains, their industriousness a shining example of doing one thing at a time.

When Aphrodite returns the next morning, she is surprised to see the task completed, and quickly assigns the second task: gathering golden fleece from the rams. When Psyche arrives, the rams are running around the field, butting heads, competing with one another. She's sure she'll be trampled if she tries to enter the field and grab some fleece. Sitting by the river, thinking, she receives some helpful wisdom from a reed: bide her time. "Wait until the sun goes down and they tire of their games. Then you can collect what you need from the fleece that has gathered on the tree branches through their rough play."

~ ~ ~

Through this task, Psyche learns to listen to her own rhythms, her soul. Rather than getting caught up and pulled along in the power of the moment, to take the time to figure out a path forward that both meets her goal and honours her inner self.

~ ~ ~

The third task Aphrodite assigns is to fill a crystal goblet with water from a stream that flows to and from the River Styx. It is carved into the side of a mountain, flowing from the top of a cliff, to the depth of Hades, and rising back up through a spring. As the water hisses and monsters warn her away, Psyche despairs again, seeing no way to approach the stream's edge. With this task, she receives help from Zeus's eagle. The eagle takes the goblet in his talon, flies to the middle of the stream, fills it, and brings it safely back to her. What the eagle brings is a new and wider perspective on the situation.

~ ~ ~

In his book, *She: Understanding Feminine Psychology* (2009), Robert A. Johnson explores the myth of Psyche and Eros in depth and shares his thoughts about what Psyche learns through this task: "The earthbound individual may look down into the crashing, swirling confusion and feel that there is no way to sort it all out. From this narrow point of view, she can not see clearly enough to have a workable perspective. It is at this moment that she needs her eagle vision, which has a much broader perspective and can see the great flow of life."

We too have done a lot of work on our journey to see this broader perspective. Finally reaching the summit, we discovered the bigger-picture view that encompasses the full spectrum of opposite energies and came to appreciate how they weave together in the great flow of life.

And now Psyche joins us in the final stage of this phase of our journeys.

~ ~ ~

Aphrodite, incensed that Psyche has made it this far, assigns the fourth and final task: go to Hades, fill a container with beauty ointment from Persephone, the goddess of the underworld, and return with it. This is a seemingly impossible task for a mortal, and again, she despairs. [This is a common human experience when faced with yet another challenge!] In the end, Psyche chooses to continue. Knowing she needs to die to enter the underworld, she climbs the highest tower she can find with the intention of throwing herself off.

At the last moment, the tower itself gives her the information she needs to complete her task. First, she is given directions to a hidden spot to find a pathless way to the underworld. "Take two coins with you for the ferryman, and two barley cakes for the three-headed dog." Then the tower warns her, "You will be asked for help three times, but you must refuse."

Psyche gathers the coins and cakes and finds the pathless path. When she comes to the River Styx, she gives one of the coins to the ferryman to take her across. Three times she is asked by pitiful creatures to stop and help, but remembering the tower's words, she does not stop. [When we understand our goal and ourselves, sometimes we don't have the additional energy to be able to help others, and that's okay.]

At the entrance to the underworld, she tosses one of the barley cakes to Cerberus, the guardian of Hades. As the dog's three heads fight over it, Psyche passes. Having finally made it, she meets with Persephone and asks her to fill the container with beauty ointment, which she does without question. Reward in hand, Psyche retraces her steps to return to the upper world. The second cake for Cerberus. The second coin for the ferryman. At last, she is back in the sun with her precious reward!

The reward isn't the end of the story though. The tower had reminded Psyche to never look in the box, but on her way to her final meeting with Aphrodite, Psyche succumbs to temptation. Wanting to be beautiful when she was finally reunited with her beloved Eros, she opens the box. Looking inside, she sees nothing, but she immediately falls to the ground in an everlasting sleep—some mysteries are meant only for the gods. [Remember, having grace doesn't mean that we are perfect. There will be challenges that seem insurmountable. There will be temptations. In fact, understanding that we aren't perfect is an integral part of our journey to grace. But, in this story, love triumphs in the end.] Eros escapes his mother, finds Psyche, and wipes the everlasting sleep from her eyes and back into the box. Psyche presents the container to Aphrodite, and Eros received Zeus's blessing to marry Psyche, making her immortal.

~ ~ ~

GRACE IN THE EVERYDAY

Just as Psyche was swayed by temptation even after receiving her ultimate reward, reaching this stage is not a permanent state of being. But it is now one that we've experienced, which means it sits within reach. Our lives are not static and we continue to learn and grow and change. Therefore, we need to continue to do the work to maintain our self-awareness. The people in our lives continue to learn and grow and change, so we need to stay in tune with the rhythm of our relationships.

What does this look like day-to-day? Most days, it looks like family members confidently pursue learning in any of its forms—including more formal classrooms— without getting caught up in the trappings of the system. We choose to participate in the environment and take from the experience what we are interested in. We evaluate the experience against our personal goals, which often include more than just grades.

When I'm stymied trying to figure out how to come up with a plan that meets the needs of everyone involved, it looks like me openly asking my children for their suggestions, knowing they too will consider everyone's needs. They are full members of the family, and they often have a fresh perspective and some pretty great ideas!

Unschooling—life—is a practice. Each day, each moment, we can choose to reach for love, kindness, and compassion. To live gracefully with others.

LIVING
UNSCHOOLING

THE TREK BACK

WHEN THE ORDINARY WORLD CALLS.

After choosing to accept the call to adventure, we have spent a lot of time and effort on this unschooling journey of personal exploration, learning, and growth. The unknown world we set out to discover now feels like home. And with our quest accomplished, it's time to enjoy the fruits of our labour.

We see our kids making solid choices, exploring their boundaries, and learning like crazy. We love spending time with them: sometimes deeply focused and in the flow of an activity; sometimes relaxed and laughing, enjoying their company; and other times commiserating and consoling and validating their frustration and sadness. It's living as a full contact sport—energizing and tiring and beautiful.

REFUSING TO RETURN

Yet, it's here that we might begin to stagnate. Life feels wonderfully satisfying in our unschooling bubble. Safe. The bubble has been so incredibly helpful as we navigated the deschooling phase of our journey. It gave us the time and space we needed to observe and contemplate how real learning happens, to better understand ourselves and our children, and to explore ways to live together as a family. And now that our unschooling lives are flowing reasonably smoothly, it can be tempting to stay in the warm embrace of our new comfort zone.

Maybe it's mostly our home. Maybe it includes regular gatherings with the local unschooling community—park days or gym days. Maybe it includes the library and the rec centre. Eventually though, as our family continues to explore and learn and grow, it's likely that we'll start to bump up against the edges of our bubble. There are interesting things in the ordinary world!

When that happens, the thought of returning to the challenges you've left behind can be intimidating. Maybe you're worried about your children experiencing the judgement of others more directly. Maybe you're wondering if you'll get caught up in the rush of busyness again, and feel pressured to prove to others that unschooling is a good choice for your family. We are reminded of all the questions and challenges we've worked through to get to this point: Will our newly won wisdom sustain us in the swirl of the conventional world?

Not only that, the process often isn't as simple as just stepping back out, as many hero stories attest. This return phase of the journey can be as intricate as our departure into the world of unschooling was. We'll need to figure out ways to re-integrate with the ordinary world that work for our family. Maybe we're feeling excited to share with others what we've learned on our unschooling journey. Maybe we're happy to concentrate on living our unschooling lives.

Our responsibility is first and foremost to our family—what works for us as individuals. So, the question to consider at this stage is whether or not our unschooling bubble continues to be a supportive and helpful feature in our journey landscape. If it's still an integral part of our lives, we will refuse to step out. At least for now. The key is to pay attention to when it starts to feel constricting. Is anyone starting to feel like they're wilting rather than growing?

There are other journeys, other mysterious worlds to be explored, but they'll wait until we're ready. And we'll soon discover that we can retreat and cocoon in our unschooling bubble whenever we feel the need to recharge.

BRINGING BACK THE GIFT OF UNSCHOOLING

Once we've chosen to begin our return journey back to the ordinary world, it can take many forms. Sometimes we may feel like we're bringing back this amazing secret with us—our lives are so much more joyful now and we want to tell anyone who will listen!

There are many tales in which the hero, having triumphed and won the reward, wants to quickly bring it back to the world for the betterment of humanity. For example, there are many stories surrounding the discovery of fire, like the Native American Creek tale, "How Rabbit Brought Fire to the People" (Brown 1993).

~ ~ ~

In the beginning, there was no fire, and when winter came, the people were cold. They knew that the Weasels on the island had fire because they could see the rising smoke and they wanted some to keep warm. The people asked the animals how they might get some, and Rabbit was the only one brave enough to try. He explained that every night the Weasels build a big fire and dance around it, and he could join them and steal some fire.

Rabbit put together his clever plan, and before he swam to the island under cover of darkness, he rubbed his head with pine tar, making his hair stand up. That night he joined the Weasels dancing around the fire, and as the dancing got faster and faster, Rabbit bowed his head deeply near the fire. As he planned, the pine tar in his hair caught fire, and he quickly ran away.

The Weasels chased him, but he was too quick. They watched from the shore as Rabbit swam back, his head ablaze. The Weasels called on the Thunderbirds to make it rain and put the fire out, but clever Rabbit hid in a hollow tree until the rain had passed. And that is how Rabbit brought fire to the people.

~ ~ ~

Rabbits appear in folk tales around the world, often as tricksters, like in this tale where Rabbit tricked the Weasels to steal some fire from them. Did you hear stories of Peter Rabbit growing up? He seemed to always manage to escape Mr. McGregor's clutches. Or watch Bugs Bunny cartoons? Bugs always got the best of Elmer Fudd when he was hunting rabbits. And at this point in our journey, we too might be feeling a bit of the trickster energy, like we're getting away with something by not doing what everyone else is doing.

The myths surrounding the discovery of fire are apt for this stage as well. In stories, fire often represents knowledge and warmth, and spiritually, our inner light. A campfire invites people to gather, cooking food and telling stories. And if we feel like we're bringing back the gift of unschooling to the world, we may want to share our stories and experience with others. Maybe we choose to more actively answer questions in online unschooling groups, or host play times or coffee chats with other unschoolers in our home, or organize camp-outs, or even conferences. Modern versions of hanging out around the campfire and sharing stories.

MAKING A FRESH START

Another way our return journey may play out is by inspiring us to make a fresh start. We may find the conventional world giving us a rather hostile reception as if we've done something wrong. They probably weren't very vocal about it while we were cocooning, busily exploring and learning about unschooling, but that can change as we return and more actively engage with the ordinary world. You may find family or neighbours dropping by regularly and, maybe even inadvertently, belittling you and your children. With people quizzing your children and questioning you, you may be left feeling inadequate, and it can take hours or even days for everyone to recover their joyful unschooling momentum.

In other words, sometimes there are people in the ordinary world who don't want you to bring your funky new lifestyle and ideas into their bubble of conventional society. So much so that they will actively lash out at you. In this case, if you find you—or anyone in your family—feeling unsafe, you may choose to escape to safety.

Maybe the flight is more metaphorical as you choose to actively distance yourself from discouraging family and friends, but some unschoolers do physically move away to distance themselves from negative environments. This may be a difficult decision to make. I can also imagine the incredible sense of relief and joy and adventure an unschooling family might feel when they choose to move to a new community—a fresh start to go hand in hand with their new perspective on learning and living.

WHEN THE ORDINARY WORLD COMES KNOCKING

Yet another way our return journey may begin is by being pulled back to the ordinary world by others. We have done a lot of personal soul searching and paradigm-shifting work to reach the summit of our unschooling journey and obtain our reward, and we may want time to rejuvenate. And then there's a knock at the door.

It may be friends or family, asking to get together. Maybe we've been avoiding social gatherings for a while, almost automatically replying with a gracious "No, thanks."

But we can take a moment to honestly consider it. Maybe the thought doesn't seem so daunting anymore. We can ask our spouse, our children—What do they think?

In another interesting unschooling twist, maybe it's our child knocking from the inside, looking out to the wider world. Be sure to listen for it. My children loved the unschooling cocoon we created for many months, but eventually, feeling safe and secure with their home base, they began looking to follow their interests beyond the embrace of our family. Lissy found Girl Guides, Michael wanted to explore karate, and Joseph wanted to expand his gaming world online, connecting with other players around the world. Of course, not all at the same time. When they were ready.

It's important to watch out for whether we continue to cling to our unschooling bubble to the detriment of our children's exploration of the world. Sure, we can bring lots of the world to them, but when they are interested in venturing out, we want to support that too.

And something else to consider: it can be tempting to seek out and favour unschooling, or at least homeschooling, communities when looking for opportunities for our children. Sure, we hope to find a more comfortable environment surrounded by families with similar perspectives on learning, but that doesn't mean our children's personalities and level of interest are going to mesh well with the group. We may find a homeschooling guide or scout troop, or homeschooling rec classes, or a server full of unschooling gamers—and it's great to try them out—but don't expect that things will go smoothly just because the other children don't go to school either. Our children aren't usually looking to connect with others over unschooling—that's our interest. Just as kids in a school classroom don't find being local and the same age very fertile ground for friendship.

People—children and adults—enjoy connecting and engaging with others around their interests. The interest itself is the key parameter, not the lifestyle of the other participants. So be open to trying out several different environments for a particular activity to find one that meshes well with your child.

Whether the outside world comes knocking, or your child is keen to begin exploring beyond your doorstep, the key to choosing when to begin the return phase of your unschooling journey is to be aware and attentive.

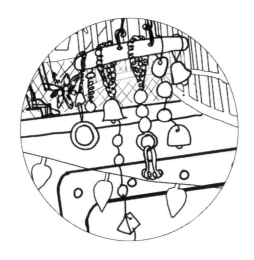

~ STAGE FOURTEEN ~

CROSSING THE RETURN THRESHOLD

INTEGRATING OUR NEW-FOUND PERSPECTIVE
INTO EVERYDAY LIFE.

No matter the motivation behind your return, as you step across the threshold back into the ordinary world, you may not quite know what to expect.

Our perspective on daily life has changed since we began our journey, as have our relationships with our children. Not to mention the joy that infuses much of our days.

We may find some people are taken aback by us, a bit confused by our hands-on approach to living, the zest for life that can often seem to ooze out of even our older children. They may be a bit resentful of how much fun we're having and how happy and easygoing our relationships seem. Don't we know life is hard?

In the sense that they mean it, yes, we do. And therein lies one of the interesting challenges of our return.

USING THE LANGUAGE OF THE ORDINARY WORLD

As we move more and more into the ordinary world, we can sometimes struggle to express our new-found perspective in words that others will understand. It can also be challenging sometimes to get into the flow of a conversation. Questions posed to us are often phrased for yes or no answers. In groups, we're expected to pronounce good and bad judgements quickly and in alignment with conventional wisdom. To do otherwise marks us as different.

At the same time, we recall how these opposites are not exclusive but complementary. We see the wholeness and real-life experience that dynamically flows between those poles! But how might we express that in a mundane conversation about whether or not our child is allowed to call us from camp? Finding the right words can be surprisingly difficult.

And how might we describe our multi-faceted lives in the more black and white terms that others will understand? While we describe our children as choosing what they want to learn, most people see children who never want to learn anything. Why the discrepancy? Because in their world view, the only learning topics that count are those in an approved curriculum and the only way to learn is to be taught by someone, preferably a teacher. So much of the learning that we see, they dismiss outright. In fact, they probably see children actively avoiding learning. When we say that we don't have bedtimes, they envision chaos and crankiness. And from their perspective, if they were to just drop the rules and leave their kids to their own devices—which is what they think we're suggesting—there's a good chance they would find themselves in exactly the spot they fear.

We are using familiar words to describe our lives, but they have a richness to them that we discovered on our unschooling journey. This richness is invisible when viewed through conventional filters. Where they see anarchy and parents leaving their children to flounder and fail, we see strong and connected relationships and parents actively supporting their children as they explore the world.

What they don't see is our active and engaged presence. They don't see parents and children living together as trusted and respected individuals. And, why would they? That's not the conventional family environment they would expect. We've just completed a long and sometimes challenging journey to understand and appreciate the unschooling way of life; it's likely they have not.

It's valuable to realize that our words are interpreted by others through the lens of their life experience. They aren't wrong—it is their truth.

THE TAO TE CHING

Legend says that when Lao Tzu was eighty years old (usually dated around 6th century BCE), he decided to seek solitude. Riding a water buffalo, he eventually arrived at the western border of China. The chief guard recognized him and asked that he write down his wisdom and teachings before he left. Lao Tzu agreed, returning a few days later with the short text that would eventually become known as the *Tao Te Ching*.

Roughly translated as "The Way of Virtue Book," or just, "The Way," one of its central themes is the interconnectedness of all things expressed through the principles of yin and yang. It encourages the development of self-awareness to understand human nature and the interconnectedness of all people, leading to a strong sense of being in the world. And interestingly, even though it was written more than 2,000 years ago, Lao Tzu begins his work by explaining the challenge of using everyday language to try to describe metaphysical concepts and questions. The language obstacle isn't new.

One of the many well-known quotes from the *Tao Te Ching* is

Simplicity, patience, compassion.

These three are your greatest treasures.

Simple in actions and thoughts, you return to the source of being.

Patient with both friends and enemies,

you accord with the way things are.

Compassionate toward yourself,

you reconcile all beings in the world.

See how well that connects with what we've been learning on our journey? So much of what we've discovered as we live and learn with our children is about being human in our world. Simplicity in actions and thoughts is possible when we understand ourselves so well that who we want to be in our thoughts and who we are in our actions are in alignment. When we are patient with both friends and enemies, we can meet them where they are, like with our language conundrum. And when we are compassionate toward ourselves, we see the wholeness and interconnectedness of all beings and treat them with kindness.

Simplicity, patience, compassion. These are some of the gifts of the hero's journey.

MAKING CHOICES IN THE EVERYDAY

So, why are we returning to the ordinary world? To expand our horizons, and our children's. The world is a wondrous place!

There are people who share our interests, people who know things that we would love to know, and people who have skills we would love to learn. So often they are happy to share their knowledge with anyone who is interested. And when there's a shared interest, the importance of age fades. At the dojo that Michael attends, there is a wide range of ages at all belt levels, and they train together. When Lissy volunteered at the animal shelter thrift store, she made a wonderful connection with a retiree around costumes and photography. Lissy ended up visiting her home to borrow some amazing clothes and props for shoots, and was regaled with wonderful stories. And for Joseph, age is not obvious in online in games and forums—knowledge and skill come to the forefront.

As we go about our days, when people realize our children don't go to school, what we bring to the world is the knowledge that the conventional wisdom around learning and parenting isn't the only way. That seed is planted inside every person we encounter—no matter how that particular moment unfolds. We exist. And if or when they are ready to consider what our children's joyful lives might say about their understanding of learning and education and parenting, they'll do so. At some point, they may even become curious enough to ask us questions—they might be hearing the first faint calls of their own call to unschooling.

I've had a few occasions when a parent at Michael's dojo knew we were homeschooling and asked me a few questions. I find those conversations so invigorating! They stretch my mind and my skills as I try to meet the person where they are and find the words that will connect with them there, and—with that connection made—find more words to take them to where I think they want to go. Because so often the question they ask isn't exactly what they want to know. It's that language thing again.

For example, when they ask, "Do you give them tests?" often what they really want to know is, "How do you know they're learning?" So, instead of giving them an in-depth rundown of the legalities of reporting, I might reply, "No, I don't. Tests are useful in classrooms because teachers have thirty-odd kids and it's the most efficient way to see what they know, but at home, I only have three kids, and I hang out with them all the time. They ask me questions, so I know what they're thinking about, and I help them find answers. I hear them using new words in our conversations, and sharing new ideas. I see them using new skills. I don't need to test them because I see their learning in action."

I get to meet the other parent where their experience is—in school—and then walk with them into my home, where unschooling lives. And since they're ready to ask questions, often they're ready to hear the answers. Their eyes light up with understanding, and they excitedly ask the next question, and the next. A few times, though both of us had been on our way out after dropping our kids off, we found ourselves in the lounge at the back of the dojo chatting animatedly until class was over. Another seed planted.

It's also helpful to remember that, just as conventional isn't synonymous with right, unschooling isn't necessarily a good match for every family. What's truly valuable is knowing there is a choice. When we feel forced to do things, so often we do them reluctantly, without much consideration or effort. It's like we give our power away. But when we choose to do things, we are more engaged and thoughtful in our actions. Even if school is a part of a family's lives, it needn't be their master—if they take the time to consider it and choose not to give the system that power. School is not the work of childhood. Knowing that they are free to choose the environment in which their children learn will encourage people to consider their unique family's needs and explore what works best for them.

These worlds—unschooling and ordinary—are illustrative, not literal. Returning to the conventional world isn't about converting or convincing others to join us. It's about integrating our unschooling lives into our ordinary world. In Lao Tzu's terms, it's about living the Way in our daily lives.

Unschooling is living.

~ STAGE FIFTEEN ~

BEING OURSELVES IN THE WORLD

FINDING THE BEAUTIFUL IN THE MUNDANE.

In the last two stages, we've talked a lot about the two worlds—the unschooling/unconventional world and the ordinary/conventional world—and how we're working to knit them together. Joseph Campbell calls this stage "Master of the Two Worlds": it is the master's ability to pass back and forth freely between them.

We certainly find ourselves spending time in both: sometimes we choose to spend time in the ordinary world with its conventional perspective and expectations; and other times we're immersed in our unschooling world, hanging out at home or with other unschooling families. As we continue to pass back and forth, we gain more and more skill with the transition.

MASTERING THE TRANSITION BETWEEN WORLDS

One thing I found helpful, especially before going places with a more conventional atmosphere and expectations, was to talk with my children before we went. They appreciated knowing what to expect so they didn't feel out of the loop. I'd let them know if there was a schedule to things, what the rules and expectations were, who else was going to be there, and so on.

For example, if we were going to the Science Centre, we'd look up the live shows that were available that day and see if there were any we'd like to try to catch. We'd talk about how we might need to leave an exhibit to get there in time to get a seat, and how we could go back to it after. I'd ask if there were any exhibits they wanted to be sure to visit and we'd put them first in our plans. I'd also mention if we were meeting up with anyone else so they knew if we might be waiting in the lobby for a bit before heading in. We'd talk about how busy it might be, depending on whether it was school trip season, and how the students usually left by 3 pm, giving us less busy time later. Or, if it was September, how it was likely to be much less busy. Knowing we'd be staying together, we might bring something for them to play with if one of them was done with an exhibit while the others were still occupied.

These prep plans and conversations would only take a minute or two in the flow of our day, maybe the morning of the visit, or a couple of days earlier, depending on the child's preference.

And then after we got back, or maybe on the drive home, we'd talk about what went well, any hiccups we encountered, and how we might approach—or avoid—them next time. Those tidbits come up naturally as we chatted about the visit. Maybe the electricity demonstration was lots of fun and they want to be sure to go again next time. Maybe we waited too long before breaking for lunch so we had some cranky moments and we decide to eat a snack just before we leave next time.

Same for visits with extended family. If there was going to be a meal at a certain time and snacking beforehand was frowned upon, I'd let them know what the plan was. I'd explain that I'd let them know when the meal was almost ready, and then when we were there, I'd help them transition from their play to the table. We'd chat about who was going to be there so there were few surprises or disappointments.

And for me, I'd be sure to have a few conversation starters handy for chatting with the other adults, like asking about their favourite TV show, and ways to change the subject if things started to go off the rails, like the trusty, "Pass the bean dip, please," we talked about earlier. I enjoyed asking questions about their interests and what they've enjoyed doing lately. People who are passionate about something are often a lot of fun to listen to! And sometimes, when they answered that they weren't really interested in anything, the question still served to plant the seed that following our interests has value.

I'd also bring toys and games so the kids had fun things to do. And if the adults were willing to join them, it was a more relaxed and fun way to enjoy each other's company. For example, we'd bring Bingo to my in-laws because it was a game we enjoyed that extended family were likely to join us to play. Either way, I was happy to play with the kids. It meant we were having fun and staying out of the way.

I'd share some ideas with the kids too. "Grams just got back from vacation, we can ask her about her trip." Or, "After lunch, we can ask Grandpa if he wants to play Crazy Eights. He likes to play that with you." I've called my Mom before a visit to let her know that the kids are really into a certain game at the moment and ask if she'd be interested in playing with them. If so, we'd bring it. If not, I'd let the kids know, and we'd come up with something else to do.

Navigating the transition between our unschooling world and the ordinary world doesn't mean we are different people—we can be ourselves in both worlds. But this planning time helped things go more smoothly and be more fun. It was also a great way for us to learn more about each other's needs, as well as the constraints, peculiarities, and customs of the places we were going and the people we were with.

THE PARRS LEARN TO LIVE IN BOTH WORLDS

Have you seen the film *The Incredibles* (Bird 2004)? At the beginning of the film, we are introduced to the Parr family. Bob Parr, aka Mr. Incredible, was a superhero back in the day before an avalanche of lawsuits against superheroes forced them all into retirement and full-time ordinary lives. Talk about constraints! We meet Bob now, fifteen years later, looking much older and working in a corporate cubicle at an insurance company. Ever the hero at heart, he surreptitiously helps an old woman to get her claim approved, but his boss finds out and berates him for not keeping the company's best interests first and foremost.

Next, we meet his wife, Helen Parr, aka Elastigirl, as she arrives at the principal's office for a meeting regarding their ten-year-old son, Dash. Dash is being disruptive in class. Again. And though he escapes punishment, it's clear he's using his superhero speed to pull pranks in class. Talking to his mom after, he reminds her that if he could just go out for sports, he'd be happy. His mom reminds him that the world just wants them to fit in and he'd be too tempted to use his powers to win.

Then we meet their fourteen-year-old daughter, Violet Parr. She watches a boy she has a crush on walk by, but when he turns around to look at her, she's disappeared. Literally.

When they all come home for dinner that night, it's clear that they are having a hard time being supers and suppressing that side of themselves to live full-time in the ordinary world. Bob is not engaged with his family and misses his old life, and Dash and Violet would rather not have their powers if they can't use them.

And now let's skip to the end of the film, after they've undergone the bulk of their hero's journey. Mr. Incredible has learned that he loves his family deeply and being with them has been his greatest adventure. And the family has learned that, together, they are a powerful superhero team that can defeat the villain.

After a three-month time skip, we learn how well the Parrs are doing now that they're able to live freely in both worlds: Dash is on the track team and, with his family cheering him on from the stands, races to a close second in the hundred-yard dash. Violet, running into her crush in the stands, doesn't shy away. Instead, she arranges a movie date with him. And when, at the end of the day, a new villain appears at the stadium, the family dons their masks, ready save humanity again as The Incredibles.

They are now able to move comfortably between their two worlds—their two identities—happy with who they are in both.

THE SPIRIT OF THE EVERYDAY

One of the challenges at this stage of our journey is that we can get caught up in thinking of our unschooling world as more meaningful and the conventional world as more banal.

As I began venturing more regularly out and about, I had a tendency to see unschooling as my inner world (not really surprising after having sparked such an intense inner journey) and the conventional world as my outer world. This meant that I saw my inner world as more meaningful and my outer world as more banal. But, just as the Parr family discovered that their lives in the ordinary world are as integral a part of themselves as their superhero lives, we too can find that wholeness.

As I explored the crossover between my inner and outer worlds more deeply, I found ways to bring my inner perspective into my outer world interactions, and I was amazed at how different things looked! I realized my views on life and living had changed so fundamentally that it changed how I approach every moment. In both worlds.

Everything seems both more mundane and more wonderful.

Here's an example. Something as mundane as tidying up a room is no longer a philosophical struggle against what else I could be doing with my time. Nor do I worry about what message it might send to the kids. With no expectations of ourselves or others, I finally felt free to choose—and in that freedom, I discovered that, for me, the choice is really about possibilities. What might unfold on the fresh canvas of a tidy room? Newly invigorated children's play? Relaxed adult conversation? Engaged family play, with adults and children sharing the stage? A rest on the couch with tea and a story?

And to boost the fun factor—since I was no longer feeling put upon and grumbling—sometimes I might listen to music or audiobooks or podcasts. Other times, I'd quietly let my thoughts wander, feeling almost meditative in the repetitive physical motions. Or, I may decide to take a nap instead, knowing that a messy room is filled with past joy and that the Lego village might inspire another bout of play before it's set aside. In these moments, living in two worlds, I've found joy, both in the moment and in future possibilities.

I was delighted to find the spiritual world mingling easily with the physical world. It turns out, the everyday tasks of life are not frustratingly mundane; there is such beauty in them when I'm open to it.

Let's try another example—the other way this time—starting with something that sits at the spiritual core of unschooling: learning. With unschooling, we have come to realize that there is learning in everything our children do. As we watch our children in action we can practically see their minds at work, the sparks of connections flashing across their face as they try out different pieces of the puzzle, searching out that one piece that will so satisfyingly fall into place. Yet, if we look at that moment through conventional eyes, we see that they are "just" doing a puzzle. At the heart of one of the most beautiful and spiritual tasks of being human—learning—so often lies the most ordinary of things. A puzzle. An insect. A TV show. A star in the sky.

Passing back and forth between my inner and outer worlds no longer seems so intimidating. In fact, these worlds enhance each other. We feel so much lighter! Free to stretch ourselves and explore beyond our comfort zones, while at other times, to say no, without judging either choice. Both are what worked for us in the moment. Moving beyond our expectations and fears, we can more clearly see ourselves, our children, and our choices.

We realize now that when a challenge arises, it's not about giving in or giving up but about releasing our need to control things, allowing us to start fresh and be open to the many possibilities that are truly present in each moment. We can hold on for the ride.

And that brings us full circle to the stories above. The possibilities that are opened up by our seemingly tedious tasks—like tidying a room. The possibilities for play and learning and joy that are inherent in the most ordinary things. Now when we look around, we see possibilities everywhere.

With our new-found perspective, we see both the beauty in our physical world and the ordinary in our spiritual world. It's all so compelling! And soon we find ourselves comfortably flowing between them. We have moved beyond yet another pair of opposites to wholeness, though this time at a different level.

These two worlds truly are one world, full of possibilities.

~ STAGE SIXTEEN ~

THE FLOW OF OUR UNSCHOOLING LIVES

LIVING AND LEARNING AND GROWING.

One of the most fundamental insights I've had on my unschooling journey is that we—children and adults alike—are always growing and changing. We see it in our children and, as our self-awareness grows, we recognize it in ourselves as well. We are not what we have been led to believe. Children are not just adults-in-the-making and adults are not finished.

We are growing and changing. Living and learning. Being and becoming. This constancy of change seems to be a foundational idea about the human experience, regardless of the era in which you live. Before we embarked on our unschooling journey, being told that change is constant probably sparked a sinking feeling in our gut, indicative of a generalized fear or worry about the future. *Oh no, what's going to happen next?* We so often assume the worst.

But as we come to appreciate change as our lifelong bedfellow, we soon recognize it everywhere. It is the sparkle of possibilities. It feels like a weight has been lifted and we are able to appreciate the moment.

LIVING OUR BLISS

This refreshing perspective frees us up to fully engage in our lives. Even challenging moments feel less paralyzing because we realize their transience. Able to breathe, we can more easily find that moment, that beat, between action and reaction where we can see the bigger picture and use it to light our path, to see the possibilities.

Campbell calls this stage "Freedom to Live," and rightly so. Almost paradoxically, our ability to fully live in each moment grows as we stop holding onto it so tightly. We know in the depths of our soul that life flows; through both calm and turbulent waters. Sometimes we're the rock being polished, and sometimes we're the leaf bobbing on the surface. We can be both. Whatever the circumstances call us to be.

And what's even more beautiful is that we begin to recognize this flow of life in others. We more clearly see the stage they are at on their journeys. We feel less judgmental and more compassionate. Their choices, their actions and reactions, say more about where they are on their journey than they do about us and ours. Our journeys are our own.

This is so freeing when we're out and about—we can be ourselves. Our upbeat attitude carries a spark of our joy into the ordinary world. When you and your family are out and about, you are a shining example, even without words, that there are possibilities and perspectives that lie outside the conventional life.

Over the years, so many people have come up to me and the kids to comment on how whenever they see us we always seem to be smiling. People we don't know but who frequented the same places we did. And it's not because our lives are somehow easier; it's because of how we inhabit our lives.

What are the fundamental characteristics we've developed or strengthened on our unschooling journey that help us embrace the joyful flow of life? I think these are some of the valuable ones:

- We're comfortable in our skin, regardless of how others see us.

- We're comfortable making choices and open to where they may lead.

- Because we aren't attached to the outcome (no expectations), our sense of self isn't riding on what happens next. We feel centred. We can be ourselves.

- We're patient, giving things time to unfold. We know there may be possibilities we have yet to envision.

- We know we will always have more to learn. Things will go awry. We will change and grow.

Our entire unschooling journey can be summed up in these five words: Unschooling is learning is living.

And that living is trusting and engaged. Aware and patient. Kind and compassionate. That is the flow of our unschooling lives.

THE ILLUSTRATED JOURNEY

1. Ordinary World

2. Dreams

3. Transitions

4. Learning

5. New Perspective

6. Joy

7. Compassion

8. Grace

9. Gifts

10. Flow

AUTHOR'S NOTE

LIVING AND LEARNING AND GROWING.

Whew. I almost can't believe we're here.

The journey of this book has taken three years. As I mentioned in the introduction, it began in January 2015 as a series of blog posts about my unschooling experiences through the lens of the hero's journey. Six months later, the series was done yet I could *not* stop thinking about it. Rather than satisfying my curiosity, it fed it until it had grown into an all-out passion! And I needed more.

I began to envision a book. I was keen to go back and revisit the stages, knowing now what I'd figured out by getting to the end of the series. I wanted to weave in story examples to create more possibilities for connection and deeper understanding, which entailed many delightful hours of research and reading.

And then, in mid-2016, I came across and connected deeply with Hema's art. As part of my research, I had found many illustrations of the hero's journey, and soon I could not shake the idea of illustrating the unschooling journey. I reached out to Hema, and we soon began a delightful side quest to explore ways to do that in her beautifully whimsical and intricate style.

And then more thoughts began weaving through my mind. Like, this is not a "how to" book. No two paths to unschooling take the same twists and turns. There is a lot of personal contemplation and processing involved as we explore and integrate these ideas into our lives. And that I wanted us—writer and reader—to take this journey together. I wasn't trying to create a top-down, teacher-student relationship, but to cultivate a conversation between us.

It was at about this point that I began envisioning the print edition of the book as a journal—with colouring pages for contemplation, lined pages for writing down thoughts, and even blank pages for doodling and sketching. Inspiration grew as I recalled my family's love for the book, *Dragonology: The Complete Book of Dragons*, edited by Dugald Steer. (A quick peek online, and Amazon informs me that I purchased it on November 11, 2004.) *Dragonology* is a beautifully illustrated book presented as the journal of famed dragonologist, Dr Ernest Drake, containing all the knowledge he managed to gather about these rare and secretive beasts. I got goosebumps as I imagined a journal filled with your own experiences and flourishes, making it uniquely yours. That means that each print copy of the book out in the world will be different from every other one. How cool is that?

I know how helpful it has been for me on my journey to look back on my thoughts from weeks, months, and even years earlier. I was reminded of insights I had gleaned but soon lost track of, maybe in a recent swirl of busy-ness. And I came across questions I had been asking myself just a few months earlier to which I now had solid answers. When I sometimes felt like I was barely treading water, a look back reminded me of the learning and growing that was slowly, but surely, happening. Often, it was just the ticket to re-energize me. Maybe you'll find that too.

What I've discovered through this project is that, while the book is (finally) done, my fascination with the unschooling journey is as strong as ever. As is so often the case, when our story begins, what we want and what we need are two very different things. When I began my unschooling journey, what I *wanted* was to learn how to create an unschooling learning environment for my children that would replace school. What I *needed* was to learn and grow as a person so I could create a fulfilling life that included my children as equal and whole human beings.

It turns out that the essence of the hero's journey is about the exploration of what it means to be human.

It's important that the journeys we chose to take feel meaningful to us. Those who undertake a journey from a sense of obligation will mostly be going through the motions. When we freely choose our path, our sense of self grows as we move forward. We discover that no experience is a waste of our time. That the challenges, the crises, and the transitions we find ourselves navigating all have value as we process and integrate them into our understanding of ourselves, our children, and our world.

Joseph Campbell talks about finding your bliss and following it. Not because that is what will be easy, but because that is what will be meaningful to *you*. Which means you will tenaciously fight your way through the tricksters, the monsters, and the many other obstacles you'll encounter on the journey to get to the kindness, compassion, and grace that lies ahead on your path.

The unschooling journey is a splendid example of a hero's journey that can be deeply meaningful for those who choose to embrace it. I am honoured that you invited me along as an ally on your journey. Thank you. And remember, have fun!

BIBLIOGRAPHY

Allers, Roger, and Rob Minkoff, dir. 1994. *The Lion King*. Burbank, CA: Walt Disney Pictures.

Anderson, Hans Christian.

Babauta, Leo. 2015. *Essential Zen Habits: Mastering the Art of Change, Briefly*. Pipe Dreams Publishing.

Bird, Brad, dir. 2004. *The Incredibles*. Burbank, CA: Walt Disney Pictures.

Brown, Dee. 1993. Folktales of the Native American: Retold for Our Times. NY: Holt Paperbacks.

Campbell, Joseph. 2008. *The Hero with a Thousand Faces*. San Francisco Bay: New World Library.

Coyne, Shawn. 2015. *The Story Grid*. Black Irish Entertainment.

Dalai Lama. 1990. *Dalia Lama: A Policy of Kindness*. Boulder, CO: Snow Lion Publications.

Gopnik, Alison. 2016. *The Gardener and the Carpenter: What the New Science of Child Development Tells Us About the Relationship Between Parents and Children. New York: Farrar, Straus and Giroux*.

Gottschall, Jonathan. 2012. *The Storytelling Animal: How Stories Make Us Human*. Boston, US: Mariner Books.

Holt, John. 1983. *How Children Learn*. New York: Delacort Press.

———. 2013. *Escape from Childhood: The Needs and Rights of Children.* MA: HoltGWS LLC.

Howe, David. 2011. *Attachment across the Lifecourse: A Brief Introduction*. London, UK: Palgrave MacMillan.

Johnson, Robert A. 2009. *She: Understanding Feminine Psychology. NY: Harper Collins.*

Kaufman, Scott Barry. 2017. "Embrace the Uncool: Brené Brown on Overcoming Shame." *The Psychology Podcast, January 11.* https://heleo.com/conversation-embrace-the-uncool-brene-brown-on-overcoming-shame/12402/

Laricchia, Pam. 2012. *Free to Learn*. Erin, ON: Living Joyfully Enterprises.

Laricchia, Pam. 2014. *Free to Live*. Erin, ON: Living Joyfully Enterprises.

Lucas, George, dir. 1977. *Star Wars: Episode IV – A New Hope*. San Francisco, CA: Lucasfilm and Twentieth Century Fox.

Madsen, Annette. 1999. "Count Lucanor by Don Juan Manuel as Inspiration for Hans Christian Andersen and Other European Writers." In: *Johan de Mylius, Aage Jørgensen and Viggo Hjørnager Pedersen (ed.): Hans Christian Andersen: A Poet in Time*, ed.. Johan de Mylius, Aage Jørgensen, and Viggo Hjørnager Pedersen. *Papers from the Second International Hans Christian Andersen Conference 29 July to 2 August 1996.* Odense, Denmark: The Hans Christian Andersen Center, Odense University, Odense University Press. 576 pages, Odense, Denmark 1999.

Popova, Maria. 2015. "The Wisdom of No Escape: Pema Chödrön on Gentleness, the Art of Letting Go, and How to Befriend Your Inner Life." *Brain Pickings*. January 19, 2015. www.brainpickings.org/2015/01/19/pema-chodron-the-wisdom-of-no-escape/.

Robinson, Sir Ken. 2006. TED Conference. www.ted.com/talks/ken_robinson_says_schools_kill_creativity/details

Vogler, Christopher. 2007. *The Writer's Journey: Mythic Structure for Writers, 3rd edition. San Francisco, CA: Michael Wyse Productions.*

ABOUT PAM LARICCHIA

Pam Laricchia is a long-time unschooling mom from Ontario, Canada. Her three children left school back in 2002, and she's been happily exploring unschooling ever since.

Pam has written a number of books about the fascinating things she's learned about unschooling and parenting over the years, as well as many articles published in various magazines, including Toronto Life, Natural Parent Magazine, Life Learning Magazine, and the Journal of Unschooling and Alternative Learning (JUAL). She's also spoken at unschooling conferences across North America and hosted the Toronto Unschooling Conference for six years.

Pam's website, livingjoyfully.ca, is the hub of her online unschooling presence, including her popular weekly podcast, Exploring Unschooling, with more than 100 episodes in its archive.

Connect with Pam online:
livingjoyfully.ca/contact
facebook.com/livingjoyfullywithunschooling
youtube.com/livingjoyfullywithunschooling

OTHER BOOKS BY PAM LARICCHIA

Get your FREE introductory book, *What is Unschooling?*, here:
livingjoyfully.ca/what-is-unschooling

Free to Learn: Five Ideas for a Joyful Unschooling Life
Free to Live: Create a Thriving Unschooling Home
Life through the Lens of Unschooling: A Living Joyfully Companion

And these translations of *Free to Learn:*
Libre d'Apprendre (French)
Libre para Aprender (Spanish)
Szabadon Tanulni (Hungarian)

Find more information about all of Pam's books here:
livingjoyfully.ca/books

Printed in Great Britain
by Amazon